THE GOD OF THE GROWING EDGE:

WHITEHEAD AND THURMAN ON THEOLOGY, SPIRITUALITY, AND SOCIAL CHANGE

BRUCE G. EPPERLY

Energion Publications
Cantonment, Florida
2025

ISBN: 978-1-63199-929-1
eISBN: 978-1-63199-930-7

Energion Publications
1241 Conference Rd
Cantonment, FL 32533

enerion.com
pubs@enerion.com

TABLE OF CONTENTS

This book is dedicated to my "good ancestors," my teachers, pastors, and friends, who live on in me and inspire me each day, in particular, John Akers, George L. "Shorty" Collins, Allan Armstrong Hunter, and the ancestors who inspired this book and guided me through the years, Alfred North Whitehead and Howard Thurman.

CHAPTER ONE

THE GROWING EDGE INCARNATE

Look well to the growing edge! All around us worlds are dying and new worlds are being born; all around us life is dying and life is being born. The fruit ripens on the tree, the roots are silently at work in the darkness of the earth against a time when there shall be new leaves, fresh blossoms, green fruit. Such is the growing edge! It is the extra breath from the exhausted lung, the one more thing to try when all else has failed, the upward reach of life when weariness closes in upon all endeavor. This is the basis of hope in moments of despair, the incentive to carry on when times are out of joint and people have lost their reason, the source of confidence when worlds crash and dreams whiten into ash. The birth of the child — life's most dramatic answer to death — this is the growing edge incarnate. Look well to the growing edge![1]

The vigour of civilized societies is preserved by the widespread sense that high aims are worthwhile. Vigorous societies harbour a certain extravagance of objectives so that people wander beyond the safe provision of personal gratifications...

---

1   Howard Thurman, *The Mood of Christmas* (New York: Harper and Row, 1972), 23. (In the course of this text, I have sought to update, with gratitude, the language of Thurman and Whitehead to include, as much as possible, all readers.)

the perfection of life begins resides in aims beyond the individual person in question.[2]

I first discovered Alfred North Whitehead and Howard Thurman as a college junior in 1972 and I have been re-discovering them ever since. The Vietnam War was at its height even though candidate and then President Richard M. Nixon promised peace. I was uncertain of my future spiritually and professionally. After initially choosing not to register for the draft, I finally decided to register, and found myself entered in the upcoming draft lottery. Mine was a low number and it was inevitable that I would be drafted. I was uncertain whether I could stay in college, receive a conscientious objector deferment, or that my request for alternative service would be rejected and I would then face military service. Canada was also an option, although I feared what would happen to me as a twenty-year-old if I left my family and friends. As I pondered the future, filled with uncertainty, I was looking for a vision. To my relief, I was granted conscientious objector status and was assigned to an alternative service position near the college. But, the quest for a theological and spiritual vision still called me forward.

I had returned to Christian faith as a first-year college student two years earlier after learning Transcendental Meditation in October 1970. My faith was amorphous with few boundaries and definitions. I was a Christian and also a Hindu and a Platonist in spirit. To be honest, I am still influenced by Hinduism and Hindu practices I learned in college and read process theology through the spirit of Plato. I saw Christianity primarily as a lifestyle that inspired social activism. I practiced Transcendental Meditation twice daily but didn't have any interest in prayer or Christian meditation. I didn't even know at the time that there were Christian mystics. I was in search of an adequate theology, philosophy, and spirituality to nurture my spirit and provide a contour for my professional studies and personal life.

2   Alfred North Whitehead, *Adventures of Ideas* (New York: Free Press 1933), 288,289.

My philosophy professor Marie Fox spoke of her friendship with philosopher Charles Hartshorne and his wife and greatest advocate Dorothy and the impact of Anglo-American philosopher Alfred North Whitehead on Hartshorne's thought. In the fall of 1972, pastor John Akers invited me to enroll with him in a seminar on Alfred North Whitehead, taught by Richard Keady, a recent addition to San Jose State University's Religion faculty and student of John Cobb at Claremont Graduate School. I signed up for the Spring 1973 Whitehead seminar, bought my text books at the Spartan Bookstore, and have never looked back.

Whitehead, along with Plato, became my philosophers, and process theology as taught by John Cobb, Bernard Loomer, and David Ray Griffin became my theological perspective. In Whiteheadian process theology I found a God I could believe in and a pathway to integrate my global spirituality with a commitment to the way of Jesus and my emerging Christian faith. Whitehead's influence led me to enroll at Claremont Graduate School in 1975, study under John Cobb, David Ray Griffin, and Bernard Loomer, and has inspired a career spanning five decades joining theology, ministry, spiritual leadership, and social action.

In 1972, I also discovered Howard Thurman, the African American mystic, activist, and pastor when he was invited to speak at our congregation, Grace Baptist Church, in San Jose, California. Thurman was the guest of the Baptist College Chaplain, George L. (Shorty) Collins. Rev. Shorty (called "Shorty" because of his height of 6 foot 5 inches, although he seemed much taller to me) was a giant in the Bay Area peace community. Both in their seventies, Thurman and Collins had been friends for five decades, having first met at a Fellowship of Reconciliation peace conference in the 1920's. Rev. Shorty introduced Thurman to the writings of South African peace activist, feminist, and anti-racist Olive Rose Schreiner. Schreiner soon became one of Thurman's spiritual mentors. As I listened to Thurman's after dinner talk, I was captivated by Thurman's gentle spirit, his slow and deliberate speech, and the wisdom he shared. In the months and years ahead,

I devoured Thurman's work, often rotating books by Whitehead, Thurman, and other process theologians. Thurman's writing was a balm for my spirit. In Thurman, I found a truly Christian mystic and discovered the connection between spirituality and social action. Thurman opened the door to a lifetime of studying and practicing Christian mysticism. In the creative synthesis of Whitehead and Thurman, I found a spiritual and theological path that joined head, heart, and hands.

I was grateful to have the opportunity to hear Thurman speak again in 1977 at Scripps College, one of the Claremont Colleges, in Southern California. A student at the Claremont Graduate School, I sought to combine Thurman's integration of spirituality and social justice with Whitehead's metaphysical vision. Once again, synchronicity struck: one of Thurman's closest friends for over five decades, Allan Armstrong Hunter, lived in Pilgrim Place, in Claremont, California, a retirement community populated by pastors and professors. A Congregationalist minister, pacifist, and spiritual guide, Hunter met Thurman in the 1920s through their involvement in the Fellowship of Reconciliation. Much to their surprise, they had been assigned to the same room containing only a single bed. In their close quarters, they spent the night coming to terms with issues of race and religion, and as a result of that "chance" – or was it providential? – encounter now over a hundred years ago, they became lifelong confidantes and companions in the quest for global peace. Synchronously, as a result of her involvement in the Fellowship of Reconciliation, Hunter became one of my wife Kate's spiritual mentors, teaching her the importance of spiritual formation for peacemaking. Kate had heard Thurman speak at a regional Fellowship of Reconciliation retreat. Through Hunter's relationship with Kate, Hunter along with Collins and Thurman, became a spiritual mentor in joining contemplation and social activism. I remember and give thanks for this holy trinity of good ancestors, Thurman, Collins, and Hunter, each day in my predawn walking prayers.

This text is an homage to the theological and spiritual wisdom of Whitehead and Thurman. Yet, more than an honoring of the past, I believe that the theological and spiritual companionship of Whitehead and Thurman is an important resource for contemplative activists in our time. These days call for a spiritual growing edge, a vision of reality and contemplative practices, that support the quest for Shalom and planetary survival in our personal and political lives.

For Thurman and Whitehead, God is the growing edge in a world of conflict and injustice. The growing edge invites us to imagine a God of Tomorrow when many cling to outmoded images of God and human existence.[3] We need their large spirited theology and spirituality for just such a time as this. In a time in which many cling to a small spirited Christianity and equally small spirited politics, we need persons of stature, theological and spiritual mahatmas, like Thurman and Whitehead, to provide wisdom for persons seeking healing, wholeness, and peace. We need their lives and teachings as an alternative world view and practical spirituality to the individualistic and violent theologies that have led to environmental destruction and climate change denial, growing isolationism and xenophobia, rising racism, Islamophobia, and anti-Semitism, hostility toward immigrants, incivility, and authoritarianism in politics and religion. We also need the example of large souled persons, inspired by large souled visions of reality, to help us face the dangers and temptations of our own busyness and the ensuing burnout, especially among social activists. In the theological mystic Thurman and the metaphysical mystic Whitehead, we find a pathway that joins the spirituality and social activism essential for our own well-being and for our care for those whose political viewpoints and policies we vehemently oppose. In their joining of philosophy, theology, and social responsibility we find a lively open-spirited, socially active progressive theology for the "living of these days."

---

3   Bruce Epperly, *The God of Tomorrow: Whitehead and Teilhard on Metaphysics, Mysticism, and Mission* Gonzales, FL: Energion, 2024),

This text emerged from the confluence of a course I was teaching on Howard Thurman, sponsored by Ellyn Sanna, publisher of Anamchara Books, with a book I was completing on Whitehead and the Jesuit paleontologist, theologian, and mystic Teilhard de Teilhard de Chardin. I am an intuitive writer, trusting the wisdom of my inner life and inspiration from the world around me for guidance and perspective in my writing. For a number of days, I had felt a deep inner movement to write about Whitehead and Thurman, mirrored in the melodies of bird songs that greeted me each morning. As I wandered through my Potomac, Maryland, neighborhood, I heard the birds chanting, "Write this! Write this!" Although the birds might have had another meaning in their morning chants, I followed the guidance I received from their morning choruses knowing that the metaphysical vision of Whitehead and the spiritual wisdom of Thurman would provide illumination and insight for activists and seekers in their quest for a healing vision for our time.

This book is an intellectual journey, but more than that it is a personal and spiritual adventure. It is also political in nature, since it is impossible to separate politics, spirituality, and theology from one another. The words of this text emerge from over fifty years living with Whitehead and Thurman and recognizing their importance in shaping my spiritual life and theological world view. Inspired by Whitehead and Thurman, my life has become a holy adventure, an adventure of ideas and spiritual growth. My hope is that these words inspire your own holy adventures.

While committed to rigorous scholarship in the writing of this text, I also embraced the wisdom of insights, intuitions, and spiritual experiences to "channel" the spirit of Whitehead and Thurman. Although they spent most of their lives in the twentieth century, I sought to see the 2020s through their eyes and awaken to how they might experience our world and how their insights might provide spiritual wisdom for our perilous yet exciting time. In some cases, my imaginative and personal as well as scholarly approach inspired me to go beyond their words to imagine how they might view certain issues – climate change, White Christian nationalism, and our current political incivility – that confront us today. To paraphrase church historian Jaroslav Pelikan, we need the insight and inspiration of the "living faith of the dead" far more than unbending authoritarianism of the "dead faith of the living" as evidenced in the science denying, binary, backward looking, divisive, and often racist perspectives of many who claim to uphold Christian "orthodoxy" today.

This text is a work of love and gratitude. I am grateful to John Akers, who was instrumental in my discovery of both Thurman and Whitehead and his mentoring of me as a young theologian. I am grateful to "Shorty" Collins for inviting Thurman to Grace Baptist Church and to Thurman for saying "yes" to the invitation and setting my feet on a never-ending spiritual journey. Together, Akers and Collins are pivotal in my lifelong integration of theology, ministry, and social change. My theological and philosophical "good ancestors" John Cobb, Marie Fox, Richard Keady, Bernard Loomer, and David Griffin live on in my work and my writing reflects my internalization of the wisdom I first received from them five decades ago. I also give thanks for the insights of C. Anthony Hunt, my colleague at Wesley Theological Seminary, for his bibliographical help and solid Thurman scholarship. In all things, I give thanks for my father Everett, whose evangelical faith was large-spirited and supportive of his more progressive son, and for my mother Loretta's fierce love. While my writing never took me away from my family as it does for some authors, every page reflects my journey with Kate, my love for my son, daughter-in-law, grandsons, and the students and congregants over the past five decades.

One final note, I unknowingly began this book on April 10, 2024, the day on which Pierre Teilhard de Chardin died in 1955. Later that day, Professor Cristobal Serran-Pagan reminded me on Facebook that Howard Thurman died 26 years later on April 10, 1981. Perhaps that is why the birds were singing joyfully that morning as if to remind me to "look well to the growing edge." In

a similar synchronicity, I sent off the manuscript of this text to my
editor on Juneteenth, June 19, the commemoration of the ending
of slavery and the final statutory enforcement of the Emancipa-
tion Proclamation in Texas. A holy adventure awaits us with a
Loving God and diverse creation companioning us.

Awakening to God's Growing Edge

Whitehead and Thurman share the belief that our world
views, spirituality, and ethics are interdependent. Whitehead asserted that the great religions began with mystical experiences and
that the love of wisdom is inherently mystical and valuational.
Thurman claimed that mystics must also be social activists, inspired by their unitive experience to seek wholeness for all persons.
Both recognized that our beliefs about God's nature and involvement in the world can promote life or lead to the death of persons
and societies. In that spirit, I will conclude each chapter with a
spiritual practice, grounded in my dialogue with Whitehead and
Thurman and a prayer by Howard Thurman. We need living and
open-spirited adventures far more than death-filled and stagnant
certainties.

In this first spiritual practice, after a time of stillness and spiritual awakening, I invite you to read Thurman's poem, "The Growing Edge," cited at the beginning of this chapter. After concluding
your second reading, take a few minutes to let the words soak in
– in the spirit of Benedictine Lectio Divina, or Holy Reading –
listening for any inspirations that may come and then contemplat-
ing their meaning for your life. What words or images stand out?
What might they mean in your life today? Then, ask the question, perhaps on a prayer walk, "What is my growing edge? What
new adventures is God calling me to?" Make a commitment to
embody the wisdom you have received. Prayerfully ground your
experience in daily life.

A Prayer from the Growing Edge

Thurman was a person of public as well as private prayer, whose prayers were often written to be part of the innovative services he led at Howard University, the Church of the Fellowship of All Peoples, and Boston University. Each chapter closes with a prayer. Listen to this conversation between Thurman, God, his religious communities, and you.

> Lord, I want to be more holy in my heart.
> Here is the citadel of my desiring,
> where my hopes are born,
> and all the deep resolutions of my spirit take wings.
> In this center, my fears are nourished,
> and all my hates are nourished.
> Here my loves are cherished,
> and all the deep hungers of my spirit are honored
> without quivering and without shock.
> In my heart above all else,
> let love and integrity envelop me
> until my love is perfected and the last vestige
> of my desiring is no longer in conflict with thy Spirit.
> Lord, I want to be more holy in my heart.[4]

---

4   Quoted in C. Anthony Hunt, *Blessed are the Peacemakers: A Theological Analysis of the Thoughts of Howard Thurman and Martin Luther King, Jr.* (Lima, OH: Wyndham Hall Press, 2005, 61-62.

CHAPTER TWO

A TALE OF TWO MYSTICS

As a child, Whitehead had "a great deal of free time. Much of it was spent outdoors…He had more time than a schoolboy would have had for solitary wondering about everything he saw." Later in life, Whitehead asserted that "he was no good unless he had a couple hours each day in which he could go off by himself and think."[1]

I could sit my back against its trunk, and feel the same peace that would come to me at night. I could reach down in the quiet places of the spirit, take out my bruises and my joys, unfold them, and talk about them. I could talk aloud to the oak tree and know that I was understood. It, too, was part of my reality, like the woods, the night, and the pounding surf, my earliest companions, giving me space.[2]

Speaker of the House Tip O'Neill (1912-1994) once remarked that all politics are local. On the one hand, we are children of the universe, connected with the Big Bang, the evolving earth, the sustenance of the four elements, and the impact of human history. On the other hand, we are also rooted in a particular time and place. The finite is Infinite and the Infinite is in the finite. The

---

1   Victor Lowe, *Whitehead: The Man and His Work*, Volume I (Baltimore: Johns Hopkins University Press, 1985), 32-33.

2   Howard Thurman, *With Head and Heart* (New York: Harcourt Brace and Company, 1979), 9.

whole universe conspires to create each moment of experience, as Whitehead says. Our creativity emerges from the interplay of freedom and tradition, and intentionality and environment. What we do with our conditioned creativity radiates across the universe and finds its home in the Memory of God.

My personal interplay of local and global shapes, as both Whitehead and Thurman would attest, every word I have penned in this text. I am a Christian theologian, spiritual teacher, and pastor, in good measure, because of the influence of my parents, especially my Baptist minister father Everett and the evangelical church of my childhood. I have been struggling with and expanding on this legacy my entire life. Although influenced by American Transcendentalism, Hinduism, Buddhism, Taoism, and the eclectic new age movement, I am whole-heartedly Christian and have been an ordained minister, teaching and preaching the Gospel since 1980. I honor Gautama and Lao Tzu, Plato and the Vedic sages, but Jesus is my personal companion and savior. I am a Reiki healing touch teacher and master but I understand Reiki through the lens of Jesus' healing ministry.[3] Moreover, I am open and affirming of the wide diversity of human experience. I am white, male, heterosexual, North American, middle class, well educated, and a member of the Medicare generation, living in the 21st century and not the first. By choice, and to some extent destiny and locality, I am politically and theologically progressive, contemplative, committed to religious and human diversity, mystically oriented, and shaped by my interests in world religions. All these are lenses through which I experience the world. They are not limitations unless I choose to fixate on them as the only lenses through which God is revealed in my life and the world. In fact, as Whitehead says, limitations of concrete existence are the source of possibility.

---

3   For more on reiki healing touch see Bruce Epperly, *The Energy of Love: Reiki and Christian Healing* (Gonzales, FL: Energion, 2017) and *Reiki Healing Touch and the Way of Jesus* (Kelowna, BC: Northstone, 2005).

Creativity and adventure emerge from concrete moments of time and place. There are unique moments and places, fully incarnational settings described by the Celtic sages as "thin places," but there are also "thin places everywhere." God is present and revealed in all things, but we always experience God uniquely in our time and place. As mystics throughout the ages have recognized, the center is here and the center is everywhere. This is the case with the insights of Alfred North Whitehead and Howard Thurman, whose messages for the ages were delivered from a certain time and place.

Alfred North Whitehead and Howard Thurman grew up in very different words and as children faced very different possibilities and limitations. Thurman grew up in the racist, violent, and spiritually bankrupt world of "Jim Crow" South in Daytona Beach, Florida. He knew hate first hand and the worst hate often came from those who called themselves "Christians." He experienced daily the soul-numbing limitations of being seen as less than human and unworthy of ethical consideration. Still, as poet, author, and mystic Maya Angelou proclaims, he rose. He became one of the most important spiritual voices of the second half of the twentieth century. Whitehead was raised in privilege with the expectation of greatness. Yet, he also rose beyond the parochialism of even the most privileged childhood to become a philosopher who counseled world loyalty beyond nationalism and self-interest. Each was a child of their origins, deeply influenced by race and class, and each also transcended the impact of their beginnings spiritually and intellectually.

From Thurman, I learned how to join contemplation and action. In reading his meditations, I discovered the world of Christian mystics and prophetic healers. From Whitehead, I found a God I could believe in and, as my teacher John Cobb says, a Christ for our pluralistic age. I read Whitehead through the eyes of Thurman's American experience of spiritual transcendence in a racist society. I read Thurman through Whitehead's vision of an adventurous God whose circle of love embraces and inspires everyone, without exception. Thurman and Whitehead inspire us to creative perseverance in the quest for the Beloved Community that is the heart of God's vision of Shalom for all creation.

Whitehead's Privilege, Pain, and Pivotal Moments

Whitehead was to "the intellectual manor born." His family wasn't wealthy but, in contrast to Thurman's family, they had all the resources and status that came from being well-educated, upper middle class, and professional at a time in which Great Britain was at the height of its global impact and power. With all the self-assurance of Gilbert and Sullivan, Whitehead's ancestors could boast, "I am an Englishman." Indeed, Whitehead and his immediate ancestors were "British Brahmins," urbane and educated with bright futures ahead of them. It was assumed that young Alfred would be a clergyman, educator, administrator, or politician.

Born in Ramsgate, England, on February 15, 1861, the son of an Anglican minister and school master of the Chatham House Academy, established by Whitehead's grandfather, also an Anglican priest, Whitehead had from an early age a proclivity for mathematics and the sciences. As a child, Whitehead, like me, went on pastoral and administrative rounds with his father and, I suspect, young Whitehead often sat at table with Anglican priests and bishops visiting at their family home. Whitehead studied mathematics at Trinity College, Cambridge, and then taught at his alma mater Trinity College from 1884-1910. He was liberal in politics and championed the equality of women in higher education, including the admission of women to Cambridge University, at the time a losing cause. He gained notoriety as a mathematician as a result of his collaboration with his former student Bertrand Russell in writing the three-volume text on the foundations of mathematics and symbolic logic, *Principia Mathematica*, published between 1910 and 1913. Whitehead concluded his British academic career as an administrator at the University of London. At the University of London, Whitehead encouraged a break from the strict class system of the past by supporting "young people from every social grade" to enter the University. In commenting on making education available to the working class, Whitehead asserts that "all this was a new factor in civilization. But the learned world is immersed in the past."[4] Throughout his life, Whitehead believed that treasuring the past was an invitation to novelty in the present and the future and not an excuse for returning to the illusory memories and social conventions of "the good old days."

Although there is little known of Whitehead's religious experience or theological perspective in his early writings, he once responded to a question posed at a gathering of the Apostles, the school's elite conversation society: "Shall we transcend our limitations?" with a mystical aspiration, "I want to see God."

On more than one occasion, Whitehead affirmed that philosophy begins with wonder. Born to privilege, Whitehead had a great deal of free time as a child, much of which was spent wandering outdoors. He loved solitude and perhaps learned early in life that religion and solitude are intimately connected. In quiet moments in the countryside, Whitehead inhaled the beauties of nature, and came to experience the world in the spirit of the Romantic poets who influenced his spiritual and intellectual life. Perhaps, in these youthful perambulations, Whitehead caught a glimpse of the God he was to write about as a mature philosopher.

Whitehead married Evelyn Wade in 1890. They were yin and yang to one another: the soft-spoken, often retiring philosopher, and the intelligent and strong-willed woman. Alfred and Evelyn were married nearly fifty-seven years, and it is obvious that Evelyn, a person in her own right and not a marital appendage, inspired, challenged, and deepened Whitehead's professional and philosophical life. Whitehead often acknowledged, as I do in my marriage, the significance of his marriage in shaping the contours

---

4   Alfred North Whitehead, "Autobiographical Notes," in Paul Arthur
     Schillpp, *The Philosophy of Alfred North Whitehead, Library of Living Philosophers*, Volume 3 (Evanston, IN: Northwestern University Press, 1941), 12.

of his intellectual life. According to the philosopher, "the effect of my wife upon my outlook on the world has been so fundamental, that it must be mentioned as an essential factor in my philosophical output...her vivid life has taught me that beauty, moral and aesthetic is the aim of existence, and that kindness, and love, and artistic satisfaction are among its modes of attainment."[5]

For a period of eight years during his tenure at Cambridge, Whitehead took a great interest in theology. He even thought of converting to Roman Catholicism. His religious explorations were described as:

> all extracurricular, but so thorough that he amassed a sizable theological library. He dismissed the subject and sold the books. A Cambridge bookseller was willing to give quite a handsome figure for the collection. It then appeared that the pay must be taken in books at his shop. So he went on an orgy of book-buying until he had overdrawn his account.[6]

Two moments, one professional, the other emotional, proved to be turning points in Whitehead's life, challenging him to re-evaluate and expand his vision of reality. The collapse in the early twentieth century of Newtonian physics, which had been presumed to be the final word in describing the universe, rocked Whitehead's intellectual world and beckoned him to embark on a lifelong adventure of ideas. As Whitehead notes in a conversation with biographer Lucien Price:

> I have been fooled once and I'll be damned if I'll be fooled again! Einstein is supposed to have made an epochal discovery [demolishing Newtonian certainty]. I am respectful and interested but also skeptical. There is no more reason to expect that Einstein's relativity is anything final, than Newton's *Principia*. The danger is dogmatic thought; it plays the devil with religion; and science is not immune from it.[7]

5   Ibid., 8.
6   Lucien Price, *Dialogues with Alfred North Whitehead* (Boston: Little, Brown and Company, 1954), 9.
7   Lucien Price, *Dialogues with Alfred North Whitehead*, 345-346.

Whitehead's experience of intellectual disillusionment inspired him to see the interplay of self-criticism and spiritual and intellectual openness as essential to the practices of religion, philosophy, and science. Even Einstein needs to be updated and the new physics overhauled and supplanted by the insights of even newer physics. A constant openness to deconstruction is necessary as a prelude for creative transformation in religion, philosophy, politics, science, and culture. World views and religious beliefs need to be constantly open to transformation as we encounter new experiences and scientific data. We must constantly update our ideas of God in light of the dynamics of an evolving universe and our growing experiences of science, medicine, and pluralism. Dogmatic finality in our religious and scientific adventures may lead to censorship and violence in our public lives, not to mention intellectually euthanizing the living God. To be faithful to God we must, as Whitehead counseled, "release Noah's dove" into an uncertain and changing world, leaving the windows of our minds open for new inspirations and welcoming novel, and sometimes disturbing, information and inspiration. God is often the source of order, but God is also the ultimate iconoclast, bidding us to let go of old certainties and deconstruct formal and inflexible fundamentalisms to experience the fire and wind of the Spirit in our time.

Personal tragedy marred Whitehead's privileged intellectual life. World War I brought the death of his aviator son Eric, and the loss of a generation of young men, many of whom were his students and younger colleagues. Many who returned from war suffered grievous injuries, including undiagnosed post-traumatic stress. In the wake of such carnage, the mathematician Whitehead may have been inspired to seek something eternal in our perpetually perishing world and find meaning in the vision of a divine companion, who treasures our lives, "the fellow sufferer who understands."[8] God is the preserver of the "tragic beauty"

8   Alfred North Whitehead, *Process and Reality: Corrected Edition.* (New York: Free Press, 1978), 351.

that emerges when the dream of youth meets the painful realities of conflict, limitation, and mortality. In recognizing that our
lives and efforts are preserved in God's everlasting experience and
memory of the universe, Whitehead believes, we find confidence
to live boldly and think innovatively knowing that our lives perish
and yet live evermore.[9]

In 1924, at age sixty-three, with academic retirement loom-
ing, Whitehead chose to embark on another adventure that joined
geography and philosophy in the United States. Whitehead was
invited to join the faculty of Harvard University, where he taught
in the philosophy department until 1937. As a professor at Harvard, Whitehead was given free rein to wonder. He was invited to
pursue an intellectual life without limits: to speculate on metaphysics, intellectual history, and religious experience, grounded in
his emerging holistic vision of a philosophy of organism.

Whitehead's open spirit shaped his teaching. Education is
an adventure of ideas and Whitehead encouraged his students to
be intellectually adventurous. Victor Lowe, one of Whitehead's
Harvard students and Whitehead's biographer, whom I assisted
as a graduate student at Claremont in 1978-1979, noted that "everyone who knew Whitehead at Harvard immediately recalls his
insistence that each student pursues those investigations which ap-
pealed to his trained instincts, not those which a professor knew
to be efficiently manageable topics for theses."[10] Whitehead was
well-known for placing student creativity over rigorous grading.
Whitehead routinely gave higher marks to his students than his
Harvard colleagues. Perhaps, Whitehead, the "easy" grader, intentionally sought to give his students a creative space to achieve excellence and the grace to take intellectual chances, often yielding
innovative work.

Whitehead's creative and liberating spirit inspired scores of
students who would become the apostles of process theology and

---

9   Ibid., 351.
10 Victor Lowe, *Alfred North Whitehead: The Man and His Work (Volume I,
    1861-191)*, 58.

philosophy in North America, Great Britain, continental Europe, and now, under the influence of John Cobb, the Peoples Republic of China. He provided a world view that intellectually undergirded liberal and progressive theology and left a legacy that shaped my life and has been a mustard seed giving options to spiritual seekers questing for a creative vision of God and a God we can believe in when our previous visions of God have collapsed. This is especially the case in the Open and Relational Theology movement, pioneered by Church of the Nazarene professor Thomas Jay Oord, which in its use of Whiteheadian images of God has become a mecca for ex-evangelicals for whom faith and a compassionate vision of God still matters.

In Whitehead, spiritual seekers discovered a dynamic, open and relational vision which inspires an equally open and relational attitude toward diversity, pluralism, and novelty in our philosophy, theology, and spirituality. As Whitehead notes, looking back on six decades of philosophizing: "The vitality of thought is an adventure. That is what I have been saying all my life, and I have said little else. Ideas won't keep. Something must be done about them…the meaning of life is adventure."[11] Whitehead died on December 30, 1947.

Against the Wall: Thurman's Providential Journey

In contrast to Whitehead's privileged beginnings, Thurman's childhood and youth were challenging culturally, economically, racially, politically, and spiritually. Born in Daytona Beach, Florida on November 18, 1899, Thurman was well aware of the all-pervasive daily trauma of discrimination. The grandson of slaves, Thurman grew up in the era of Jim Crow laws and voter suppression. Thurman experienced white supremacy on a daily basis, not just among the obviously racist members of the Ku Klux Klan, but in the ubiquitous, unreflective racism, characteristic even of those whites who sought to be friendly to the black community. Whites

---

11   Lucien Price, *Dialogues of Alfred North Whitehead*, 254.

could travel freely into Thurman's neighborhood, but African Americans risked life and limb if they were found after sundown in predominately white neighborhoods. This is sadly still the case today in certain white neighborhoods where black walkers and joggers as well as motorists "driving while black" are seen as threats and treated accordingly. Like those about whom Thurman wrote in *Jesus and the Disinherited*, what may have been the first African American liberation theology, Thurman and his family lived with their "backs against the wall."

An incident from Thurman's youth that would have been unimaginable to the educated Englishman Whitehead captures the ubiquitous reality of racism that Thurman and most African Americans in the USA South daily experienced, and tragically still experience in many quarters of the USA. One autumn Thurman was hired to rake the leaves of a family that had employed his grandmother to do their laundry. As he raked leaves into orderly piles, their young daughter, perhaps four or five, playfully scattered piles of leaves that contained colorful leaves she wanted to show Howard. When Howard became frustrated and told her to quit, and then threatened to tell her father when she continued to scatter the leaves, she angrily poked him with her hat pin. In response to the assault, Howard drew back in pain. The young girl unreflectively responded, "O Howard, that didn't hurt you! You can't feel!"[12] That child's instinctive response betrayed many whites' assumption that African Americans were somehow sub-human, unable to feel the pain inflicted upon them in the cotton fields of slavery and the antebellum separation of families and in the 20th century exclusion from soda fountains, voting booths, and playgrounds. Embedded in relational and legally enshrined racist realities of Southern white privilege was the dehumanization of persons of color, reflected in the belief that persons of color were only slightly superior to the beasts of the fields. That moment of

---

12   Howard Thurman, *With Head and Heart*. Harcourt and Brace, 1979), 11-12.

"you can't feel" was one of the factors that shaped the person who was to become the mystic of empathy.

Later in life, the mature Thurman, like Whitehead, was to champion the vision of an empathetic and feeling universe in which interdependence rather than individualism characterizes the fundamental nature of reality. From his own experience of institutional and relational dehumanization, Thurman recognized that if people believe that you can't feel, they will consider you subhuman and undeserving of respect or ethical consideration. Such dehumanization even came from devout white Christians who claimed to believe the biblical affirmation that humans are created in God's image, and then restricted that image in practice to persons of European origin. Thurman the theologian and spiritual leader was to see empathy, the ability to identify with another's feelings and to recognize them as equivalent to one's own, along with the affirmation of reverence for life, grounded in the image of God residing in all persons, as essential to the quest for racial equality and social justice. From his privileged position in society, Whitehead arrived at a similar perspective, described by the philosophical term, "pan-experientialism" or "panpsychism," the affirmation that feeling is universal. Similar to Thurman, Whitehead asserted that value and experience are coextensive with reality and that each creature has value apart from their use to others. Disregard and diminishment of another's value goes against the grain of metaphysics and morality in an experiential universe.

The social and economic structure of the South stifled the dreams of people of color. Education was considered a luxury for black youth and during Howard's youth, Florida provided few opportunities for a bright young black person to advance educationally. Teenage Howard Thurman found out there were only three public high schools for black youth in the state of Florida. Thurman learned early that "separate but equal" is inherently unequal. Against all odds, and through what he felt was divine providence, the impoverished Thurman was able to attend high school,

college, seminary, and become one of America's most influential
preachers and spiritual leaders.

From the very beginning of his life, young Thurman had a
mystic sense. He felt the universe flowing through him as one
great pulse of Divine Love. He felt at one with the winds and sea.
"When I was young," Thurman recalls, "I found more companionship in nature than with people…The quiet, even the danger,
of the woods provided my rather lonely spirit with a sense of belonging that did not depend on human relationships."[13] Despite
the racist degradation of Jim Crow America, Thurman lived in a
universe in which every creature can praise God just by being itself. (Psalm 150:6) To the young mystic, "all things were one lung
through which all life breathed…a vast rhythm enveloping all, but
I was a part of it and it was a part of me."[14]

Like Whitehead, Thurman was raised in a Christian home.
Church was at the heart of his family's life. Thurman experienced
both the pettiness and grandeur of his childhood religion. Young
Howard saw through narrow orthodoxy and religious exclusivism
of his family's Baptist church. Dogmas stifle the spirit and divide
humanity into saved and unsaved. When his father, Saul Solomon
Thurman, a good and hard-working but agnostic man, died, their
Baptist pastor would not conduct his funeral or allow him to be
buried in the church graveyard. Eventually his mother and grandmother found a minister willing to preach at his father's funeral. Thurman recalls being spiritually traumatized by the itinerant
evangelist's perorations. "I listened with wonderment, then anger,
and finally mounting rage as Sam Cromarte preached my father
into hell." At that moment, Howard vowed never to have anything to do with the church.[15] While Howard's departure from the
church was short-lived, that experience of binary and exclusivist
religion shaped his theology and spirituality. Thurman proclaimed
that faith was about experience and not doctrine, and love and not

---

13 Ibid., 7.
14 Ibid., 226.
15 Ibid., 6.

judgment. A champion of global spirituality, Thurman believed that there are a variety of ways to worship God congruent with the varieties of human experience and culture, not to mention God's personal relationship with every human being. Thurman affirmed later in life that God's light shines in every authentic religion and far beyond the confines of institutional Christianity.

While Whitehead was raised on Romantic poetry and stories of his nation's glory, Thurman's spirit was bolstered by his grandmother's stories from her days as a slave. Howard remembers his grandmother, Nancy Ambrose, describing the words of a slave preacher to the gathered slave community of which she was a part. After preaching about Christ's death on Calvary, he would pause and then proclaim, "You are not niggers! You are not slaves! You are God's children!"[16] Later Jesse Jackson, one of Thurman's spiritual followers, taught young African American children to chant, "I am somebody!" No doubt, Thurman learned from his grandmother the art of persistence found in spirituals that proclaimed to the young Thurman, "Over and over, over and over, my soul looks back and wonders how I go over" and "There is a balm in Gilead that saves the sin-sick soul." Later Thurman was one of the first persons to write a book about the life transforming power of the Spirituals.[17]

The God who spoke through the wind and surf, and whispered through the leaves of the great oak tree also touched us through synchronous encounters. Thurman believed that God's providential care enabled him to attend high school in Florida, when at the time only three schools in the whole state were open to African American students, the nearest being in Jacksonville, nearly a hundred miles away from his home in Daytona Beach. To attend high school, Howard would have to live with one of his cousins. When he attempted to board the train to move to Jacksonville, the railroad official, no doubt motivated by racism, re-

16 Ibid., 21.
17 Howard Thurman, Deep River and the Negro Spiritual Speaks of Life and Death (Richmond, IN: Friends United Press, 1975).

fused to let him put his cumbersome and dilapidated trunk on the train. Thurman would have to send his trunk "express," but lacked the money necessary for the transaction. Defeated and fearing that he would not be able to continue his education, Thurman sat on the curb and began to cry. Out of nowhere, a shabbily dressed African American man appeared, asking him "What the hell are you crying about?" When Howard shared his lament, the stranger responded, "If you're trying to get out of this damn town to get an education, the best I can do is help you." He marched Thurman up to the office, paid the fee, and disappeared without a word.[18] Thurman came to believe that there are truly times when we entertain angels unaware, who provide us with what we need at the exact time we need it! God is not a supernatural *deus ex machina,* entering our lives only occasionally from the outside to perform a miracle; still, there are miracles and divine messages everywhere if we are willing to open our eyes and take a risk in trusting God's vision of justice and wholeness. Providence is an everyday reality touching everyone, not a supernatural intervention reserved for the chosen few. There are moments where we can exclaim in gratitude the words of the spiritual, "Over and over, over and over, my soul looks back and wonders how I got over!"

Thurman saw God's providence in his acceptance at Morehouse College, an historically black college, where he received not only a world-class education but a sense of dignity that transcended the indignities African Americans routinely experienced. Morehouse College's President John Hope was the mouthpiece of God's affirmation to an anxious young man.

> He always addressed us as "young gentlemen." What this term of respect meant to our faltering egos can only be understood against the backdrop of the South of the 1920's. We were black men in Atlanta during a period in which Georgia was infamous for its racial brutality. Lynchings, burning, unspeakable cruelties were the fundamentals of existence for

18 Howard Thurman, *With Head and Heart: The Autobiography of Howard Thurman* (New York: Harcourt, Brace and Company, 1979, 24.

black people. Our physical lives were of little value. Any encounter with a white person was inherently dangerous and frequently fatal. Those of us who managed to remain physically whole found our lives defined in less than human terms.[19]

Following graduation from Morehouse, Thurman became one of three African American students admitted to Rochester Theological Seminary, where for the time he found himself living as a minority in an almost completely white world. While the doors of English higher education were opened wide for Whitehead, Thurman was initially rejected by his first seminary choice, Andover Newton Theological Seminary, which at the time did not admit African Americans. Race matters, then and now, and we as a nation (the USA and other slave holding and slave trading nations) and as Christians truly have much to repent and repair in our attitudes toward race and, may I add, sexuality, economics, neurodiversity, and immigration.

Thurman had a strong sense of vocation. Indeed, Thurman begins his autobiography *With Head and Heart* with an account of his own vocational realization. Serving as an assistant minister, during the summer after his first seminary year, he received a phone call asking for the Senior Minister, who was away on holiday. The head nurse noted that there was a patient who was dying, and then asked, "Are you a minister?" Thurman describes this life-changing moment, "In one kaleidoscopic moment I was back again at an old crossroad. A decision of vocation was to be made here, and I felt again the ambivalence of my life and my calling. 'I am a minister.'" When the apprentice minister arrived at the man's room, the man had only one question, "Do you have anything to say to a man who is dying?"[20] I too have lived with this ambivalence in terms of my vocational identity. I have spent my professional life going from pulpit to classroom and study to hospital room. Like Thurman, my ministry has shaped my theology and my theology has shaped my ministry. "I am a minister"

19 Ibid., 36.
20 Ibid., 3-4.

and my ministerial vocation, as well as my multiple vocational identity, is reflected on every page of this book.

Thurman rose to prominence over four decades as a faculty member at Morehouse College, Dean of the Chapel at Howard University, pastor of America's first intentionally multi-racial congregation, The Church of the Fellowship of All Peoples in San Francisco, California, and ultimately the first African American Dean of Chapel at a primarily white university, Boston University. In each case, Thurman felt God's call to leave significant and stable positions to follow God's vision. Like Whitehead, the adventures of ideas, the call to racial healing and global spirituality, beckoned Thurman forward to embrace new and risky possibilities.

Tragically, Thurman's first wife Katie died of tuberculosis, leaving behind a young child and grieving husband. Again, similar to Whitehead, Thurman's aim at self-transcendence and professional excellence was furthered by his second wife, Sue Bailey. Equals in every way, they were married for nearly fifty years. Sue and Howard were partners, companions, and edified one another through moral and intellectual support. Thurman says of Sue Bailey, who brought into "our coming together a rare beauty of person, a clear and analytic mind, a sensitive imagination, and an enthusiasm of heart that only love can inspire." An advocate of women's rights as well as racial equality, she was an active "tennis player" volleying back and forth ideas and dreams in the marital adventure.[21]

God calls us forward to new horizons. Providence lures us forward and when we say "yes," new energies are set free for our spiritual growth and the healing of those around us. Well-established at Howard University, where in the course of twelve years, he had created unique programs in spiritual formation and contemplative worship, Thurman initially balked when in 1944 he felt the call to help found the Church of the Fellowship of All Peoples in San Francisco, California. Thurman recalls that he received guidance from a saying employed by the British War Resisters "It

---

21 Ibid., 84.

is madness to sail a sea that has never been sailed before, to look for a land, the existence of which is a question. If Columbus had reflected thus, he never would have weighed anchor, but with this madness he discovered a new world."[22] Thurman joined with a white Presbyterian minister to embrace the uncertain future, and together they created a multi-racial congregation, reaching out to artists, intellectuals, spiritual seekers, and working people of all faiths with innovative programs, joining body, mind, and spirit.

Firmly established at the Church of the Fellowship of All Peoples, Thurman once more was called to a new adventure. Like Abraham and Sarah, Howard and Sue Thurman left the familiar to return to the east coast, where Thurman accepted the position of Dean of Marsh Chapel at Boston University and Professor of Spiritual Disciplines and Resources at the Graduate School of Theology. The journey was painful. It involved leaving beloved friends and an innovative congregational program. But, when we recognize that God is with us in our travels, our lives become a holy adventure in which we share in God's dream for us and the world.

Whitehead and Thurman both saw God's aims present as lures for adventure calling us forward to embrace creative and unanticipated possibilities. Thurman saw divine providence guiding his steps, inviting him toward new horizons and uncharted territories. After retiring from Boston University, Thurman returned to San Francisco, where he established the Howard Thurman Educational Trust, dedicated to support African American college students, both intellectually and spiritually, especially in the Deep South. Thurman's holy adventure from "Jim Crow" Daytona Beach to global acclaim was part of a never-ending story. God is at work in our cells and souls, and despite the challenges we face and the machinations of those who try to keep us down, God guides our pilgrimage toward the far horizons of faithfulness and freedom. Thurman died on April 10, 1981. On April 10, 2024, I unknowingly, but synchronously and providentially, penned the first words of this book.

---

22 Ibid., 140.

Awakening to God's Growing Edge

Whitehead and Thurman both believed that each moment was grounded in the moral and spiritual arcs of the universe. While both enjoyed solitude, they also recognized the importance of relationships in our personal growth. They were grateful for their teachers and mentors, who were embodiments of naturalistic providence which undergirds our lives, whether or not we recognize its presence.

Good Ancestors. We all stand on the shoulders of others. Whitehead says that the whole universe conspires to create each moment of experience. While this may seem abstract, another approach to the graceful interdependence of life is to remember those whose wisdom and love have brought you to this point in your life. In the Yoruba religious culture of Africa, an important spiritual practice is to remember our good ancestors, those persons who have come before us who shaped our lives and the world positively and whose wisdom is still available to us. The Christian practice of remembering and praying with the saints is similar in spirit. We can be open to their insights and guidance for our daily lives and values. Their lives inspire us to practice "good ancestry" in our lives today by committing ourselves to the well-being of future generations, children, grandchildren, and people whom we will never meet. We are all good ancestors in the making!

Each morning, as I take my predawn walk, I remember my good ancestors, deceased and yet living on in God's realm and my life, whose lives have made a difference in my spiritual and professional development: my parents Everett and Loretta and my brother Bill and mother-in-law Maxine; my professors, including John Cobb, David Ray Griffin, Richard Keady, Marie Fox, Shunso Terakawa, and Bernard Loomer; my ministerial mentors, including two of Thurman's dear friends, George L. "Shorty" Collins and Allan Armstrong Hunter; and dear friends who have shaped my life. I also invoke the wisdom of Howard Thurman and Alfred North Whitehead as spiritual mentors and good ancestors. In remembering, I feel connected with their wisdom and awaken to new insights. Although they are no longer physically present, they live on in this text and my personal and professional values.

In this exercise, reflect on your good ancestors: What persons have shaped your life? What wisdom have you received from them? Take time to give thanks and open to their continuing wisdom.

I invite you also to give thanks for the influence and continuing impact of your good ancestors, Alfred North Whitehead and Howard Thurman, with whom we travel in the course of this text. Feel your connection with their lives and give thanks for their impact on your lives.

Conclude your spiritual practice considering how you might practice being a good ancestor for future generations. How might you contribute to a better world for them? What concrete actions can you take to promote their well-being and the well-being of future generations across the globe? We are always planting seeds for future generations, for those we may never meet and will continue the quest for justice long after we are gone. Let us plant good seeds for the future.

A Prayer from the Growing Edge

Deep down Thurman and Whitehead believe that we are all mystics. We are always standing on holy ground, waiting, albeit unaware, of the glory shining round us. Thurman records a mystical experience as a prayer.

I journeyed to a hill at the close of day
Darkness stole on the valley beneath as sleep on a tired brow
Silence pursued me all day
Won at last -
Exhausted I lay at his feet...
No sense of senses, time – space all
Around me ran together
In one expansive, streaming, liquid quiet.

Suddenly with a start – time began
The heavy cares of the years seemed lighter now -
God so near
I was radiant
With holy light.[23]

---

23 Howard Thurman, *Walking with God: The Sermon Series of Howard Thurman – The Way of the Mystics,* Edited by Peter Eisenstadt and Walter Fluker (Maryknoll, NY: Orbis Books, 2021), xix.

CHAPTER THREE

METAPHYSICS AND MYSTICISM

> [God's] purpose is always embodied in the particular ideals relevant to the actual state of the world. Thus all attainment is immortal in that it fashions the actual ideas which are God in the world as it is now. Every act leaves the world with a deeper or fainter impress of God. He then passes into his next relation to the world with enlarged, or diminished, presentation of ideal values.[1]

> As a boy in Florida, I walked along the beach of the Atlantic…I had a sense that all things, the sand, the sea, the stars, the night, were one lung through which all life breathed. Not only was I aware of a vast rhythm enveloping all, but I was part of it, and it was part of me.[2]

This chapter will be somewhat asymmetrical in approach. Whitehead was a mystical metaphysician who wrote very little on mysticism, but whose later philosophy exudes a mystical spirit, which has only recently been mined by Whitehead scholars. Thurman was a theological mystic, who disliked being called a theologian, but whose writings reveal a deeply mystical theology in which the experience of God as well as commitment to social

1   Howard Thurman, *With Head and Heart*, 152.
2   Howard Thurman, editor, An Introduction to *A Track to the Water's Edge: An Olive Schreiner Reader* (New York: Harper and Row, 1973), xxvii-xxviii.

transformation is the ground for authentic theological reflection. Although they approached mysticism with different emphases, both would agree that deep down all philosophy and theology is mystical in its emergence from experiences of the Holy. We may use different language, based on our differences in religious tradition or culture, but it is the Divine speaking through our spiritual experiences. We may also speak of God in different ways as a result of experiencing, like the sight impaired persons and the elephant, different aspects of God's nature and presence in the world. Still, deep down, whether we emphasize infinity or intimacy, eternity or change, or beauty or justice, the light of God prismatically shines through our theological and philosophical reflections, all of which touch something of God, none of which can encompass the totality of God. Both Whitehead and Thurman remind us that inflexible dogma kills and openness awakens our experiences of God. Our mystical experiences all remind us to humbly recognize that God is always more than we can imagine.

Whitehead never claimed to be a mystic and downplayed his spiritual experiences. Thurman focused on the interplay of spirituality and social change but never attempted a systematic theology or metaphysical exposition. In many ways, Thurman's spiritual focus reflected Whitehead's comments from his classic *Religion in the Making* that Buddhism is a philosophy seeking a life expression and Christianity is a life, the life of Jesus, seeking a metaphysic. While it is unlikely that the two men met, Thurman, thirty-eight years Whitehead's junior, was familiar with Whitehead's work and approvingly quotes Whitehead on the solitariness necessary for religious growth in his classic *Deep is the Hunger*. After positively noting Whitehead's statement that "religion is what a [person] does with [their] solitariness," Thurman continues: "It is the solitariness of life that makes it move with such ruggedness.

All life is one, and yet life moves in such intimate circles of awful individuality. The power of life is perhaps its aloneness."[3]

In this chapter, I will weave together the metaphysics and mysticism of Whitehead and Thurman as well as explore their points of contact as they sought to describe a universe in which experiences of the Holy are available in every moment and encounter. I will elaborate on the relationship of their spiritual visions to social change in greater detail in Chapter Five.

As we ponder the human spiritual adventure, we are like Jacob, who awakens from a dream of a ladder of angels, and exclaims:

> "Surely the Lord is in this place—and I did not know it!" And he was afraid and said, "How awesome is this place! This is none other than the house of God, and this is the gate of heaven." (Genesis 28:16-17)

In similar fashion, poet Mary Oliver counseled, "Pay attention. Be Amazed. Tell about it." The astonished and gobsmacked – or was it God smacked? – Jacob renamed the place of his epiphany, "Beth-El," the house of God. Jacob's journey with God doesn't end at Beth-El but eventuates in a wrestling match with a nocturnal spirit, whom we suspect is God. (Genesis 32:24-32) Holding on for dear life, Jacob refuses to let go of his spiritual opponent, and bargains, "I will not let you go unless you bless me." (Genesis 32:26) In their unique ways, and from the lens of their particular experiences, Whitehead and Thurman discover a God-filled world and struggle to find a life-supporting and world-affirming vision of God, in contrast to the authoritarian, coercive, and often violent images of God and the divisive religious experiences they inspire. Authoritarian visions of God lead to genocide, slavery, ecological destruction, and demagoguery while relational images of God inspire a democracy of the spirit which promotes the equality and well-being of all God's children and reverence for life

---

3   Howard Thurman, *Deep is the Hunger* (Richmond, IN: Friends United Press) , 169. I am grateful to my Wesley Theological Seminary colleague C. Anthony Hunt for this citation.

in its manifold variety. Both Thurman and Whitehead sought to
describe God in terms of love and not fear, following as Whitehead says the expansive spirit of John and not the more doctrinal
and institutionally oriented Paul.

Whitehead's Metaphysical Mysticism

Since the focus of this book is the relationship of spirituality
to social activism and transformation, I will be exploring Whitehead's intricate and complex metaphysical vision in terms of its
ability to nurture a socially responsible spirituality. It is my belief
that Whitehead's metaphysics is through and through spiritual in
orientation and that the major themes of Whitehead's cosmology
emerge from and promote spiritual experiences and positive social
change. Indeed, Whitehead sees spiritual experiences as foundational not only for religion but also metaphysics.

> Religion bases itself primarily upon a small selection of
> the common experiences of the race…religion claims that its
> concepts, though derived primarily from special experiences,
> are yet of universal validity to be applied by faith to the or-
> dering of all experience. Rational religion appeals to the direct
> intuition of special occasions, and to the elucidatory power
> of its concepts for all occasions. It arises from that which is
> special, but extends to what is general.[4]

In the following sections, I seek to provide a framework of
common ground between Whitehead and Thurman rather than
a systematic analysis of their writing. As Whitehead notes, "philosophy is akin to poetry, and both of them seek to express that
ultimate good sense which we term civilization. In each case there
is reference to form beyond the direct meanings of words. Poetry
allies itself to metre, philosophy to mathematic pattern."[5]

---

4   Alfred North Whitehead, *Religion in the Making* (New York: Meridian,
     1960), 31.
5   Alfred North Whitehead, *Modes of Thought* (New York: Free Press, 1968),
     174.

All Things Flow. Night is falling here in Potomac, Maryland. It has been a beautiful spring day, but now I am leaning toward a quiet night, a British mystery on PBS, Acorn, or BritBox, a gentle sleep, and then the brightness of a new day. As I write these words, I am reminded of a song my mother often sang at bedtime:

> Now the day is over
> Night is drawing night
> Shadows of the evening
> Steal across the sky…
> When the morning wakens
> Then may I arise
> Pure and fresh and sinless
> In Thy Holy eyes.

I suspect that Whitehead heard this hymn, written by Anglican priest Sabine Baring-Gould (1834-1924), at bedtime as well. Tucked in the midst of Whitehead's magisterial *Process and Reality* are the words of another hymn, "Abide with me/Fast falls the eventide," as an illustration of the interplay of permanence and flux.[6] For Whitehead, the process is the reality. All things flow. Seasons change. God is eternal and unchanging. God is also, as Rabbi Abraham Joshua Heschel asserts, "the most moved mover." God's fountain of love flows through all things, giving them life and purpose. Life is call and response, in which God calls and then the world flows back into God, its response to divine creativity, providing God with new possibilities for God's own adventurous creativity.

Change is real, and the unchanging finds its metaphysical and spiritual home in the constancy of flux. Although God's faithfulness is unsurpassed and unchanging, "God's mercies are new every morning." (Lamentations 2:22-24) The world of change and embodiment is not a flight from God, but the theatre of divine agency and glory. The whole changing world is filled with God's glory. Or as Whitehead says, God is incarnate in the world of change.

---

6   Francis Lyte, "Abide with Me" (1847).

The reality of change inspires us to change. The pure conservative, holding onto the past, goes against the nature of the universe. In a constantly changing world, injustice is not the final reality. Outmoded doctrines and mores give way to new insights. The same applies to political perspectives. Constitutional "originalism" and the inflexible hallowing of yesterday's political and religious achievements go against the nature of ever-evolving life and the quest for a life-supporting civilization. The worst thing we can do for a religion's or a nation's well-being is attempt to go back in literal and uncritical fashion to its founding documents. Indeed, even as some attempt to go backward in areas of globalism, human rights, or religious exceptionalism, their quest will ultimately be thwarted. You cannot step in the same waters twice. The river of life and the Source of the flow move forward despite our efforts to freeze our images of humankind and its Creator. We can – and should – give thanks for the USA Constitution and Bill of Rights and the dedication of its framers, and the insights of the Bible, for example, and follow the truths they embody, but also recognize the limitations of wisdom and ethics of the Constitution's framers as well as the outmoded science and mores of scripture just as we should confess our own moral and practical limitations. The moral and spiritual arcs never stand still, but move forward in new and creative ways, despite the wayward recalcitrance of our institutions and their leaders. The moral and spiritual arcs challenge us in our self-described progressivism to go further toward Beloved Community and the realization of God's realm "on earth as it is in heaven."

Change gives birth to hope. We are never fully contained by the present moment's injustice but can break down the barriers, self-imposed and imposed by unjust social systems, which prevent us from experiencing and sharing our full humanity. As the spiritual says, "Trouble don't last moreover." In this *Message,* Eugene Peterson renders 1 Peter 5:10:

The suffering won't last forever. It won't be long before this generous God who has great plans for us in Christ - eternal and glorious plans they are! - will have you put together and on your feet for good.

We can have our eyes on the prize of freedom precisely because in the openness of the future, change beckons us forward. While the mystic sees "time as the moving of eternity," the mystic also embraces and shapes the world of sense, embodiment, and change. Physical existence is not a prison nor is time an illusion, inferior to timelessness; rather change reflects the loving creativity of God and invites us to be change agents ourselves. Jacob's ladder of angels begins here on earth, mounts toward the heavens, and then returns to our changing world with wisdom, courage, and energy to face the challenges of each new day. The changing world lives by the incarnation of God, and our quest for justice incarnates God's ever-changing and always personal vision in the here and now and for future generations.

Everything, Everywhere, All at Once. The whole universe conspires to create each moment of experience. Interdependence is the nature of reality. Everything is connected. The Southern African word *Ubuntu,* "I am because of you, we are because of one another," describes the intricate interconnectedness of life in which our joys and sorrows are one, despite the illusion of self-made individualism. We are not alone, nor are we isolated. The vision of an interdependent universe is not only metaphysical but also spiritual and political. Deep down, God and the world are connected with one another, and each person emerges from and shapes to greater or lesser degree their social and political environment. As Whitehead notes:

> In a certain sense everything is everywhere at all times. For every location involves an aspect of itself in every other location. Thus every spatio-temporal standpoint mirrors the world.[7]

7   Whitehead, *Science and the Modern World* (New York: Free Press, 1967), 91.

In the words of environmental activist and writer Bill McKibben, the best thing an individual can do to respond to the threat of global climate change is quit being an individual. Even the most self-styled rugged individualist is a product of their environment. Even the most successful business person depends on their employees and consumers for their success. As a professor for over forty-five years, I know that my creativity depends on my students' presence and interest. As I tell my students on the first day of class, "I put together my syllabus in the privacy of my study. Now you are here, and everything's changed. We have a whole new class, different than the one I imagined!"

There is no self-made individual nor isolated nation. Creativity and artistry are real and should always be encouraged. Yet, our creativity and artistry occur only as a result of a supportive and nurturing environment and historical background. We are agents, and we can "rise" above our environments and others' perceptions of us, as Maya Angelou asserts, and still remember that our achievements and agency are communal in origin and impact.

As I write this morning, I give thanks to my "good ancestors," living and deceased, who inspired me to become a theologian, minister, and spiritual guide. I am grateful for the spiritual and educational resources my parents provided for me. I acknowledge with gratitude the impact of Kate, my wife of nearly fifty years, whose support and love enabled me to grow as a pastor, professor, writer, and person. Even in the life of a solitary predawn scholar, there is no separate reality. Everything flows into everything else. The mystic and ethicist alike commit themselves to partnering with God and the ambient and immediate creation to create a world in which justice flows down like waters and righteousness like an ever-flowing stream, so that laughter, health, and growth are realities for every child and their family. In an interconnected universe, there is no other. As poet Francis Thomas avers, "you cannot pluck a flower without stirring a star."

A Living Universe. Whitehead's metaphysics are an adventure in global re-enchantment. There is magic in the air and we can see it from the Webb and Hubble telescopes or an electron microscope. Nature is alive and throbbing with experience. Energy flows through all creation. Experience is universal. There is, as the Jesuit paleontologist-theologian Pierre Teilhard de Chardin asserts, a "within" to every existent thing. Similar to the evolutionary mystic Teilhard, Whitehead claims that the basic realities of the universe are occasions or drops of experience, complex and interdependent, each one emerging through its process of self-creation. Experience is universal and so is the creativity of each moment of experience. "You can feel" is the motto of the universe and human life and the inspiration to "do something beautiful" for God and our companions, enriching their lives and inspiring feelings of joy and affirmation. Contrary to the words of the young girl who poked Thurman, "you can hurt, you can rejoice, you can be content, and you can be restless," and these feelings go beyond humankind to the non-human world. God treasures your feelings even as God challenges you to greater empathy toward others' feelings.

Each moment arises from the universe, synthesizes its experience in a moment of experiential vibrancy, and contributes its experience to the universe beyond itself. The indigenous vision of life and spirit in all things, often disparaged by scientific materialists and avaricious capitalists as primitive, reflects the deepest nature of reality, while the lifeless world of unfeeling, inert atoms is an abstraction – indeed, an illusion grounded in ignorance and the quest for control and profit - projected onto our cells and souls. A living universe is open to and reflective of God's presence and in turn, as we shall see, shapes God's experience of the universe, providing God with both challenges and possibilities in relationship with the broad cosmic and human adventures. A relational universe reflects the empathy and connectedness of a relational god.

As I write in the predawn hours of a spring Maryland morning, my ninety-pound Golden Doodle Tucker sleeps beside me.[8] His legs are twitching as he dreams about racing across our town-

---

8   "Golden Doodle" refers to the mixed breed of Poodle and Golden Retriever.

house commons. Later in the morning, I will hum a familiar tune, and he will come to life, jumping with delight, knowing that soon he will be going to the Dog Park at the neighboring Cabin John Regional Park. When our son, daughter-in-law, and grandsons come to the house, he is filled with joy, barking, and jumping. He is fully alive, fully sentient, and open to possibility. He feels joy and he also feels pain.

Scientific studies describe trees cooperating as communities to nurture one another and flowers sending out scents to attract bees. The octopus has a soul, interacts with humans and has preferences. Crows can solve puzzles and Right Whales and Dolphins delight in playfulness. The mystic sees life everywhere. The heavens declare the glory of God. The whole earth reflects God's creativity. "All nature sings and around me rings the music of the spheres," as lyricist Maltbie Babcock exclaims.

When the Psalmist proclaims "let everything that breathes praise God," the poet is capturing the deepest liveliness of existence. The patron saint of ecology, Francis of Assisi proclaims a living universe, in which all creatures sing "Hallelujah."

> Be praised, my Lord, through all your creatures,
> especially through my lord Brother Sun,
> who brings the day; and you give light through him.
> And he is beautiful and radiant in all his splendor!
> Of you, Most High, he bears the likeness.
> Praise be You, my Lord, through Sister Moon
> and the stars, in heaven you formed them
> clear and precious and beautiful.
> Praised be You, my Lord, through Brother Wind,
> and through the air, cloudy and serene,
> and every kind of weather through which
> You give sustenance to Your creatures.
> Praised be You, my Lord, through Sister Water,
> which is very useful and humble and precious and chaste.

Praised be You, my Lord, through Brother Fire,
through whom you light the night and he is beautiful
and playful and robust and strong.
Praised be You, my Lord, through Sister Mother Earth,
who sustains us and governs us and who produces
varied fruits with colored flowers and herbs....
Praised be You, my Lord,
through our Sister Bodily Death,
from whom no living man can escape....
Praise and bless my Lord,
and give Him thanks
and serve Him with great humility.

There are "thin places," reflecting and revealing divine wisdom, everywhere in the world imagined by Whitehead, Thurman, Celtic adventurers, and First American sages. Wisdom and insight whispers to us through rustling leaves, the morning chants of birds, the mother and father love of osprey, the loyalty of our companion animals, and the ingenuity of chimpanzees. This is no anthropomorphism but reality itself in all its wondrous vivacity and energy. Behold, life abounds, we are always on holy ground. Holy ground calls us to reverence for life in all its diversity.

The Universality of Value. Whitehead proclaims that experience and feeling are universal. Life in its diversity is energetic and animated. The whole world, deep down, is God-filled. And as the Psalmist says, everything has the ability to praise God (Psalm 148, Psalm 150:6). What feels and what can praise is valuable, apart from anyone's interests. "You matter, you are of value, your experience is important regardless of what others think," is God's pronouncement on all creation.

Love is value-affirmation in action, promoting the well-being and the achievement of others' value on their own terms and for the well-being of creation. In contrast, the war maker, nationalist, ideologue, and binary thinker deny the value of others. "You can't feel" is their mantra when they consider those outside their realm of ethical and political consideration. At the heart of war-making, racism, sexism, homophobia, and all divisive behaviors is objectification and dehumanization, grounded in the denial that others have similar experiences, joys, and sorrows as us, and from the religious viewpoint, the denial of God's blessing on and presence in the "outsiders." Our "outsiders" aren't like us: their pain and delight don't matter, their sorrow and joy don't matter, they are expendable, we won't miss them, and neither will God!

While tough decisions may need to be made in politics and foreign policy, and the decisions nations may make can cause pain as well as joy, Whitehead asserts that value is coextensive with reality. Whatever can feel, human or non-human alike, is valuable to itself and to God, and should be valuable to us. Whitehead recognizes that "life is robbery," but equally challenges us to have good reasons for destroying other life forms or putting other humans at risk through war or greed. The affirmation of human rights leads to the affirmation of the rights of non-humans and the recognition that we must do all we can to bring beauty and joy to the world.

Recognizing the universality of experience and value, even when I eat fish, poultry, or meat, I need to give thanks and honor, as many indigenous people do, for the gifts of other creatures that sustain and enhance my existence. Reverence for life is the aspiration of ethics in its broadest sense. Morality seeks to promote value in every interaction. As a chant I learned at the Shalem Institute for Spiritual Formation says, "I thank you God for the wonder of my being. I thank you God for the wonder of all being." The social activist adds, thanking God for all being leads to seeking wholeness and justice for all beings.

The Artistry of Experience. Whitehead speaks of God as the poet of the universe leading it by God's vision of truth, beauty, and goodness. God is also the source, nurturer, and example of the artistry that characterizes every moment of experience. Following the example of divine artistry, you are an artist, poet, and creator in each moment of experience, and so is every other creature in the universe. Each occasion of experience inherits and embraces, positively or negatively, the world around it, including God's vision; shapes that experience in its moment of self-creativity; and contributes its moment of creativity to its successors and the future of the world beyond itself. Creativity and freedom are built into the nature of life. The world is an ever-expanding theater of creative synthesis, not a zero-sum container in which my gain is your loss, or any creaturely existence dishonors God. Freedom and creativity abound in an open and relational universe and God seeks to encourage greater and greater circles of creativity and freedom congruent with the well-being of our immediate and planetary environment. The greater the agency and creativity that occurs in a community, the greater opportunities for adventure and prosperity, in human society and the planet as a whole.

Divine or human, a good parent is both nurturing and iconoclastic. They want their child to grow, do new things, explore new possibilities, travel to the "far country" of adventure and creativity, while also enjoying the intimacy of relationships. This same intimate affirmation of freedom is God's wish for all of us and inspires our own "stride toward freedom" for ourselves and all creation. God is interested in relational novelty, newness and experience, and affirms "all the places you'll go" in the exploration of your gifts and possibilities. Centering on all of us and embracing everything that occurs, God aspires toward that same freedom and creativity at every level of life, even in a world where competition is the counterforce to cooperation in the process of evolution. Still, experience, value, and freedom are the holy trinity of each moment of life, and our aspiration in the quest for God's Beloved Community of Shalom. Unity and evolution are as equally, if not more, characteristic of reality as division and entropy.

God's Empathetic Creativity. Mystics have often counseled that the goal of human life is to embody or imitate God, to become as like unto God as possible in our finite world of perpetual perishing. Whitehead sees God as the ultimate exemplification of the metaphysical principles that characterize reality and God is the primary agent in the emergence of the universe as we know it. Reality is not only God-breathed but God-shaped in its interdependence, creativity, relationality, and quest for value in the moment and the long haul of history. For Whitehead, as for Thurman, God is the Ultimate Empath and Relativist. God feels the universe, embraces the experience and value of creaturely existence, nurtures freedom and creativity, and treasures the world of change. God is, as Abraham Joshua Heschel says, the most moved mover. God feels and cherishes our feelings. God says to us, "you can feel," encourages us to feel our own feelings and honor the feelings of others.

My Claremont teachers and mentors John Cobb and David Griffin describe God's nature in terms of "creative-responsive love." In its wondrous variety, the world lives by the incarnation of God. God enters each moment of experience as the source of possibility, the ground of each occasion's initial aim and the values and inner energy nurturing its own process of self-creation. God's power is relational, and not coercive. God inspires and shapes all things and also honors and nurtures their freedom and artistry. Like a good artist, God must pay attention to and work with the unique experiences of each creature. God may be the potter, as Isaiah says (Isaiah 45:9), but the clay is neither inert nor passive, and has qualities that even the Divine Potter must adapt to and take into consideration to promote the artistry of persons and communities.

God is an artist, poet, teacher, and loving parent, and not a dictator and distant sovereign. Guided by the power of love, not the love of power, God nurtures that same quest for hospitality, inclusion, empathy, and support in ourselves. Fluid and inclusive in love, God's circle of compassion is intimate and universal and all-encompassing and personal. Non-binary in spirit, God's love includes all creation in God's creative presence: God's graceful hospitality embraces all. While we may turn away from God's vision in the desires and devices of our hearts, promoting self-interest, injustice, and violence in thought, word, and deed, God never gives up on us. Sheep and goats are both welcomed into God's realm. "Goats" are sheep in the making, not reprobates to be discarded and damned.

We make a difference to God. The Good Parent is the fellow sufferer who understands. God feels our pain and delights in our joy. Our lives contribute to God's joy and sorrow. God feels the pain of young children in Gaza, Ukraine, Sudan, and Jim Crow South. God feels the elation of those whose right to love is made the law of the land. "Jesus knows our every sorrow. Take it to the Lord in prayer." Whitehead's God embodies in creative-responsive love the heart of William Blake's "On Another's Sorrow."

> Can I see another's woe,
> And not be in sorrow too?
> Can I see another's grief,
> And not seek for kind relief?
>
> Can I see a falling tear,
> And not feel my sorrow's share?
> Can a father see his child
> Weep, nor be with sorrow filled?
>
> Can a mother sit and hear
> An infant groan, an infant fear?
> No, no! never can it be!
> Never, never can it be!
>
> And can He who smiles on all
> Hear the wren with sorrows small,
> Hear the small bird's grief and care,
> Hear the woes that infants bear --
>
> And not sit beside the next,
> Pouring pity in their breast,
> And not sit the cradle near,
> Weeping tear on infant's tear?

And not sit both night and day,
Wiping all our tears away?
Oh no! never can it be!
Never, never can it be!

He doth give his joy to all:
He becomes an infant small,
He becomes a man of woe,
He doth feel the sorrow too.

Think not thou canst sigh a sigh,
And thy Maker is not by:
Think not thou canst weep a tear,
And thy Maker is not year.
Oh He gives to us his joy,
That our grief He may destroy:
Till our grief is fled and gone
He doth sit by us and moan.[9]

As our ultimate and intimate companion God seeks the "best for that impasse," working for wholeness and beauty in the concreteness of our wondrous and ambiguous world. The moral and spiritual arcs of history are not abstract but move through our lives and political structures one moment at a time pushing us toward God's Beloved Community of Shalom. We can turn away and halt the progress of God's vision, embodied in the moral arc moving in our lives, but God never gives up on any of us, the best of us and the most recalcitrant of us, in God's quest for beauty, goodness, love, and truth. When we turn toward justice, supplanting self-interest with world loyalty, we can feel God's heart beating in our hearts and in all creation. The mystic plunges into the world of pain and possibility knowing that God's love is embodied in the

---

9   William Blake, "On Another's Sorrow," *Songs of Innocence and Experience* (Oxford: Oxford University Press, 1977), 141.

hopes and conflicts of life and that we can become God's companions in bringing God's vision to birth on earth as it is in heaven.

Thurman's Empathetic Universe

According to Thurman scholar Luther E. Smith, Jr., "Howard Thurman resisted being called a theologian. To him, the word refers to one who attempts to describe God's nature, character, and action, often in ways that are static and abstract rather than dynamic and concrete. Thurman felt that most theological reflection ignores 1) the vitality of the religion which refuses to conform to a system of definition and description, and 2) the significance of the theologian as religious subject.[10] Thurman's theology resembles what I have described in a number of my books as "theo-spirituality," that is, reflection grounded in spiritual experiences and practices, lived encounters with God, and the interplay of the theologian's concrete social location with the movements of the God of the universe, whose presence is both infinite and intimate. Theology's primary purpose is to describe and promote God's vision of justice, wholeness, and beauty, and to create a friendly world of friendly people. And this involves living by these values in our personal and political lives, not just talking about it from the sidelines. Our theologies emerge and evolve in the maelstrom of history and our discovery that God is with us in the counter, commonplace, and creative moments of life.

Perhaps Thurman's view of theology was shaped by the trauma of hearing a preacher proclaim that that his father was going to hell because he was an agnostic. Perhaps he recognized the presence of destructive theology in the child's declaration that he couldn't feel pain when she jabbed him with a hat pin, Perhaps, he was also responding to the use of theological abstractions and biblical verses taken out of context to justify racism, slavery, dehumanization, and injustice. Much like Whitehead, Thurman

---

10 Luther E. Smith, Jr., *Howard Thurman: The Mystic and Prophet* (Richmond, Indiana: Friends United Press, 1991), 46.

saw dogmas as straitjackets, imprisoning mystical experiences and marginalizing critical alternative viewpoints. Tragically theology has been "weaponized" to condemn minority theological visions, silence protest, and undergird the unjust status quo.

I believe that Thurman would be comfortable with the approach taken to theology and metaphysics in this text: a lively theo-spiritual dialogue emerging from the interplay of mysticism, ethics, and tradition; open-ended and unfinished; welcoming of diverse voices and viewpoints; universalist in perspective; and committed to concreteness in social transformation and the equality of all peoples. For both Thurman and Whitehead, our theological reflection must embrace change and relativity, and affirm that divine revelation is present in all creation and in the varieties of religious experience and faith traditions.

While not systematic in approach, Thurman described an empathetic universe that welcomed diversity, transcended parochialism, and celebrated the personality of God and God's liberating and uniting presence in creation. Thurman's theology was grounded in, and ungirded, the "affirmative mysticism," he learned from the Quaker mystic Rufus Jones, who asserted that mysticism embeds us in the complexities of history. The world matters, bodies matter, and black bodies matter. The heavens declare the glory of God and so do the cries of each newborn baby. The mystic could be both heavenly minded in their self-transcendence and solitariness and earthy good in their commitment to seeing and bringing forth the image of God in all creation, individually and communally through political involvement. In many ways, the same elements that Whitehead sees as essential to understanding God and the world are at the heart of Thurman's world view. In the following paragraphs, I will present an outline of Thurman's world view with attention, as I did with Whitehead, to its implications for mysticism and spiritual formation.

Ubuntu, Relationship is Everything. Like Whitehead, Thurman affirms the virtues of solitude and individuality. The mystic and prophet must stand apart from the religious and social environment. In the privacy of experience, the inner sanctuary, we can "be still and know that I am God" (Psalm 46:10) and follow the beat of a different drummer than those for whom religion and politics are the drumbeat and sanction of the status quo and the bastion of backward-looking thought. Yet, like Whitehead, Thurman proclaims that life is social and that beneath the wondrous and challenging diversity of life is an intricate and interdependent unity. Life involves diversity and life is also one. According to Luther Smith, "Thurman believes that the urge toward community, toward harmonious unity in life, can be found everywhere from the smallest cell to the whole universe."[11]   Community is at the heart of the universe and our ethical lives. To be in tune with God's universe, we must go beyond isolation and fragmentation to wholeness and unity.

> If life has been fashioned out of a fundamental unity and ground, and if life has developed within a structure, then it is not to be wondered at that the interest in and concern for wholeness should be part of the conscious intent of life, more basic than any conscious tendency toward fragmentation.[12]

Although we must affirm and value our uniqueness reflected in our life experiences, decision-making, and gender and ethnic identities, no person or nation "can separate himself from his fellows, for mutual interdependence is the characteristic of all life."[13]

Our "search for common ground," the title of one of Thurman's books, is based on and inspired by the organic unity of life. While the ground of our lives aims at wholeness and justice, creativity and freedom, the realities of concrete existence are often ambiguous. Our environment can cure or kill, inspire or intimidate, expand or contract, or heal or harm. This is especially true of

---

11   Luther E. Smith Junior, *Howard Thurman: Mystic and Prophet* (Richmond, IN: Friends United Press, 1991), 49.

12   Howard Thurman, *Disciplines of the Spirit,* (Richmond, IN: Friends United Press),104-105.

13   Thurman, *The Search for Common Ground* (Richmond, IN: Friends United Press, 1986), 2-3.

societies that can choose to promote either Beloved Community
or Dystopic Divisiveness.

Thurman was a global theologian, affirming the goodness of
life and aspiring toward a friendly world of friendly people. He
also knew first hand of the soul deadening brutality of racism. The
unity of life can only be achieved experientially when we see ourselves as one and recognize that our destinies are intertwined. The
quest of embodying God's vision takes us toward rather than away
from one another and simultaneously promotes individuality and
interdependence. The truly interdependent self sees themselves in
everything else and everything else in themselves. Thurman testifies that "life is against all dualism. Life is one...against all the
things that divide within and without, life labors to meld together
into a single harmony."[14]

Bearing the Imprint of Divinity. Thurman believed that every
person reflected the image of God. The affirmation of the image
of God is a reality that promotes justice and empathy and not an
irrelevant abstraction. The denial of God's image in humankind
is not only bad theology, reflecting a demonic image of God; it
allows those in power to disenfranchise and control those whom
they see as lesser humans, while celebrating God's presence in our
lives promotes self and other affirmation. Thurman tells the story
of black preachers who were given permission by slave owners to
share the gospel with their fellow slaves a few times each year. After
relating the story of Calvary and Jesus' sacrificial love, something
every slave could understand in their cells and souls, and stripes on
their bodies, the preacher concluded, "his eyes scrutinizing every
face in the congregation, and then he would tell them, 'You are
not niggers! You are not slaves! You are God's children!'"[15]

> Thurman recalls the impact of the sermons of President
> John Hope of Morehouse University affirming the value of
> each student in his sermon messages.

---

14 Thurman, *With Head and Heart,* 269.
15 Ibid., 21.

He always greeted us as "gentlemen." What this term of respect meant to our faltering egos can only be understood against the backdrop of the South in the 1920s. We were black men in Atlanta during a period in which the state of Georgia was infamous for its racial brutality. Lynchings, burnings, unspeakable cruelties were the fundamentals for fundamentals of existence for black people…our lives [were] defined in less than human terms…No wonder then that every time Dr. Hope addressed us as "young gentlemen," the seeds of self-worth and confidence, long dormant, began to germinate and sprout.[16]

Jesus says "you are the light of the world…let your light shine." (Matthew 5:14-16) God's light enlightens everyone, and God delights in our successes and affirms our inherent wholeness. (John 1:1-5, 9) God brings forth the beauty of all creation; God also experiences all creation. "God's eye is on the sparrow and I know God's watching me," so affirms the African American spiritual. You are so important to God that God is constantly watching you. God is "at stake" in your life and decision making and God calls us to see the holiness in ourselves and every other person. You can add to or detract from God's quest for Common Ground and Beloved Community by your actions, especially in the political sphere. Decades later, one of Thurman's followers, Jesse Jackson proclaimed to inner city youth, beaten down by poverty and racism, "You are somebody. I am somebody."

I suspect that, despite his deep humility, Thurman would resonate with the self-affirmation of the Black Power chant, "Say it loud! I'm Black and I'm proud!" and would universalize that statement to embrace all persons, beginning with the downtrodden and marginalized and embracing the powerful and privileged. Self-affirmation, grounded in the image of God in all creation, recognizes the value of all creation and inspires the quest for equality and liberation for all those who have been traumatized by personal or social violence. Reverence for life includes our self-affirmation,

---

16 Ibid., 36.

and refusal to be dehumanized, as well as our affirmation of the value and worth of others. In Thurman's valuational universe, we can affirm with Rabbi Hillel, an older contemporary of Jesus:

If I am not for myself – who will be?

If I'm only for myself – what am I?

If not now – when?

Value is at the heart of reality. Self-affirmation characterizes all existence. As Whitehead notes, each moment of experience aims at its own momentary fulfillment and impact on the world beyond itself. Whatever exists and whoever exists, is energized by the great lung of the Spirit breathing through all creation, giving life and worth to each creature and calling up persons and institutions to proclaim the universality of human – and creaturely – dignity. And, so in the spirit of the African American spiritual, the marginalized and privileged can come together honoring each other's value:

I got shoes, you got shoes

All of God's children's got shoes

When I get to heaven gonna put on my shoes

I'm gonna walk all over God's heaven…

I got wings, you got wings

All of God's children's got wings

When I get to heaven gonna put on my wings

I'm gonna fly all over God's heaven.[17]

We all have shoes. We all have worth. We all have God's wings and we can fly because God loves us and even loves our enemies, and there's nothing we can do about it, except share God's valuing process with everyone we meet.

A World of Possibility. Thurman is the theologian of the "not-yet," to quote theologian Ilia Delio. Humankind and God are not yet what they shall be. There is more to each one of us than we can imagine and the sky is the limit for each child created in God's image. Tragically, racism and poverty have severely limited the pos-

---

17   19th century African American Spiritual

sibilities not only of slaves but of their descendants. Growing up in Florida where only three high schools were available to African American youth, Thurman knew the disastrous consequences of placing limits on the human adventure. He lamented that poverty constricted a child's imagination and the scope of their dreams. He also knew the love of his mother and grandmother and their sacrifice and confidence that led to his ability to go to high school, college, and seminary, and opened him to a world of possibility unavailable to most of his contemporaries in Jim Crow America. While well aware of the impact of racism and poverty on our ability to fathom the breadth of possibility, Thurman was also well aware of the soul-constricting reality that sexism placed on women. His wife Sue Bailey pushed the boundaries of race and gender in her time, claiming her ability to be fully human in a social order determined to define her as second class and inferior to her white and male counterparts. God breaks through every glass ceiling so that all God's children "got wings" and can soar!

Graceful interdependence and healthy community, in contrast, is "characterized by its ability to allow persons (and nature) to actualize their potential. In actualizing their potential, persons come to recognize their worth and purpose for life."[18] When we recognize the image of God within us, waiting to be born and mature, we take the first steps in realizing our potential. When asked to pen an article on "What Can We Believe In?", Thurman's response was "not only can I believe in myself, I must believe in myself."[19] We can believe in ourselves because God believes in us and is moving in our lives, making a way with our partnership where previously we could see no way.

Let Freedom Ring and Creativity Sing. Despite the realities of slavery, Jim Crow, and the continuing impact of racism in the United States, Thurman was an apostle of freedom. Freedom is built into the nature of reality and finds its foundation in the

---

18 Smith, *Howard Thurman: The Mystic as Prophet,* 50.

19 Howard Thurman, "What Can We Believe In?" *Journal of Religion and Health* (April 1973), 14.

movements of God in history and our individual lives. Divine providence gives birth to freedom by creating the circumstances for persons to rise above their environment and past history. God's circle of freedom embraces all of us and God is constantly pushing the boundaries of freedom in our social and political lives. God gives up on no one, whether slave or slave owner. Each person can embody a higher ideal and climb the upward path toward full humanity in God's Beloved Community. Providence is open and relational, not determined and unilateral. God is not the source of the status quo, but the energy of possibility that transcends the limitations placed on us by ourselves and others. Freedom arcs toward creativity and emerges from possibility. God is the engine of justice. Seeking and committing to justice seeking, along with peacemaking, requires an open-ended universe in which new possibilities for abundant life are always emerging.

> Always there seems to be something more to be experienced, to be felt, to know. My mind rejects any conclusion as being final. The greatest source of hope, therefore, for both the present and the future, is the awareness of the potential in me, in other people, in life itself.[20]

Moreover, God is constantly at work in our lives, calling us beyond self-interest to care for others. God provides an alternative vision that motivates us to go beyond fear and anxiety, and the personal and social evils they provoke. "God is working within us, working to overcome this spirit."[21]

In its highest manifestation human freedom, reflecting God's freedom, finds its fulfillment in loving community. There is always more toward which we can aspire. Limitation is real and yet the limits we face do not preclude creativity. The concreteness of life's limitations is also the material upon which we build a life. To-

---

20   Ibid., 117,
21   Howard Thurman, *Walking with God: The Sermon Series of Howard Thurman, volume one – Man's Struggle and the Prophets,* edited by Peter Eisenstadt and Walter Earl Fluker (Maryknoll, NY: Orbis Books, 2020), 70.

day, we might imagine Thurman, and also Whitehead, championing the disability and LGBTQ+ communities' quest to incarnate God's vision for their lives. Thurman would affirm the sentiments of Viktor Frankl, forged in the amid the genocide of Holocaust, "Everything can be taken from a man but one thing: the last of the human freedoms—to choose one's attitude in any given set of circumstances, to choose one's own way." Indeed, his manifesto and Frankl's are one: backs against the wall, we can still choose to become fully human, exercising our freedom of spirit, regardless of the actions of others.

> For I believe that there is always something that can be done about anything. What can be done may not alter the situation, but the individual may relate to unalterable situations within the context of his own choosing...a man need not ever be completely and utterly a victim of his circumstances despite the fact, to be repetitive, that he may not be able to change the circumstance. The clue is in the fact that a man can give his assent to circumstances or withhold it, and there is a desert and a sea between the two.[22]

God wants us to exercise our freedom and agency. Freedom, possibility, creativity, and responsibility are pathways through which the moral arc of history pushes us forward so that we may push history forward toward God's vision for us, our communities, and the planet.

A Personal-Universal God. Although Thurman has been described as "god intoxicated," like many mystics, Thurman experienced the Holy rather than penned a systematic account of God's nature. He didn't attempt, as James Weldon Johnson says of a slave preacher described in his book *God's Trombones,* "to unscrew the inscrutable."[23] Rather, he felt the "lung" of the universe flowing through him with insight, energy, and unity. Despite his theological reticence, Thurman affirmed that God is the primary source

22 Ibid., 117.
23 James Weldon Johnson, *God's Trombones: Seven Negro Sermons in Verse* (New York: Penguin, 2008), 3)

and exemplar of the relational, value-laden, creative, freedom loving, peacemaking, and liberative movements of life. God is the
engine of value, imagination, community, and self-affirmation,
challenging everything that places limits on human, and non-human, value and possibility. As we will discover in the next chapter,
both Whitehead and Thurman have Jesus-shaped visions of God.
I believe Thurman's most concentrated vision of God is found in
the four pages of his autobiography *With Head and Heart.* In the
next few paragraphs, I will let the mystical theologian speak for
himself and then elaborate on his reflections.

God is the source of the self-affirmation and self-worth, the
vocational consciousness of all things. Thurman would affirm the
wisdom of the saintly "heretic" Pelagius who claimed that each
newborn child bore the image of God and that God's grace en-
ables us to live out God's values in our quest for faithful companionship with our Creator. Thurman saw his mission to be an
agent of reconciliation as inspired by God's aim at wholeness for
all creation. God is the ultimate example and inspiration of our
quest for Common Good, or Beloved Community.

> It is important in this accounting that at bottom all of
> this was part of my meaning of God in common life. God
> was everywhere and utterly identified with every single thing,
> incident, or person. The phrases "the God of Abraham, Isaac,
> and or Jacob," or again, "the God of Jesus," were continuously
> luminous with me in my journey.[24]

The Infinite is intimate. The Cosmic centers each one of us.
The Eternal gives birth to the world of change. God is both universal and local, the Beyond within. Thurman experienced Jesus
as the human face of God. The incarnation was not a supernatural
act but a reflection of God's intimate love and inspiration of all
creation. Thurman notes, "I prayed to God. I talked to Jesus. He
was a companion…God was a reality. Jesus was a fact."[25]

---

24 Thurman, *With Head and Heart,* 266.
25 Ibid, 266.

God's presence is personal as well as universal. God guides our path moment by moment and over the long stretches of history. God "points the way to that which may yet await me around some turn in the road ahead." Divine providence guides our steps. As the gospel song witnesses:

> We've Come This Far By Faith,
> Leaning On The Lord.
> Trusting In His Holy Word.
> He's Never Failed Us Yet.
> Oh, Oh- Oh- Can't Turn Around,
> We've Come This Far By Faith.[26]

In speaking of divine providence, Thurman continues: "'Nothing walks with aimless feet' is not to say that I am bound and held fast by kismet or even predestination. But it is to say that all life, indeed all experience, is heavy with meaning, with particular significance."[27] God is present and active in all things moving toward the goal of community. Providence, as the African American spiritual prays,

> Guide my feet while I run this race,
> guide my feet while I run this race,
> guide my feet while I run this race,
> for I don't want to run this race in vain![28]

Thurman asserted that "God stands in relationship to all existence somewhat as the mind of man stands in relationship to his space-time existence," symbiotically related to the world, yet constantly luring the soul forward toward wider and wider circles of love and creativity.[29] God is the Deep Soul of our souls and Deep Spirit embodied in our cells. In this spirit, Thurman affirms that

---

26 Albert A. Goodson, "We've Come This Far by Faith" (1956)

27 Howard Thurman, *With Heart and Mind*, 268.

28 "Guide My Feet," African American Spiritual, believed to be written in the Reconstruction period, following the Civil Ward.

29 Thurman, *The Search for Common Ground*, 41.

the mystic vision of life captures the essence of God's relationship
to the world.

> The mystic affirms that God is the Creator of life totally,
> and that every living thing is a manifestation of that creativ-
> ity; and deep within the structure of everything is a core of
> reality which is in its essence one with that out of which all
> life comes.[30]

Thurman speaks approvingly of Danish astronomy Tycho
Brahe's vision as describing his own understanding of God's presence in the world: "There is magic all around us – in the rocks, the
trees, the minds of men…and he who strikes the rock aright may
find them where he will."[31] God's life moves through all creation,
energizing and illuminating every creature.

In God the Infinite and intimate meet. God is global and
yet personal, beyond all description (the apophatic way) and yet
revealed in each creature and in the religious adventure (the kata-
phatic way). Thurman's vision is panentheistic in spirit. God's love
is creative and is present in all things and yet God's eye is on the
sparrow, embracing the experience of all things:

> There can be no thing that that does not have within it as
> part of its essence, the imprimatur of God, the Creator of all,
> the Bottomer of existence…in all these things there is a secret
> door which leads to the central place, where the Creator of life
> and the God of the human heart are one in the same.[32]

"God in all things, and all things in God," affirms panenthe-
ism. God moves dynamically in all things as their deepest reality
and the source of possibility, creativity, and possibility. All things
are also present in God, embraced in God's loving experience of
our lives. God's knowledge of the world is not indifferent but is

---

30 Howard Thurman, *Walking with God: The Sermon Series of Howard
    Thurman, volume two – The Way of the Mystics.* Eisenstadt and Walter Earl
    Fluker (Maryknoll, NY: Orbis Books, 2021), 20.
31 Ibid., 268.
32 Ibid., 269.

shaped by God's vision of Shalom and quest for liberation. God knows "the troubles we've seen," and God works within the course of our lives and history to "agitate the comfortable and comfort the agitated." Thurman's vision of divine awareness, all things in God, can be described by one of his favorite scriptures, the inspiration of some of his most insightful meditations, Psalm 139.

> Lord, you have searched me and known me.
> You know when I sit down and when I rise up;
>   you discern my thoughts from far away.
> You search out my path and my lying down
>   and are acquainted with all my ways.
> Even before a word is on my tongue,
>   O Lord, you know it completely...
> Where can I go from your spirit?
>   Or where can I flee from your presence?
> If I ascend to heaven, you are there;
>   if I make my bed in Sheol, you are there.
> If I take the wings of the morning
>   and settle at the farthest limits of the sea,
> even there your hand shall lead me,
>   and your right hand shall hold me fast.
> If I say, "Surely the darkness shall cover me,
>   and night wraps itself around me,"
> even the darkness is not dark to you;
>   the night is as bright as the day,
>   for darkness is as light to you. (Psalm 139:1-3, 7-11)

God's knowledge and love nurture our creativity. The One whose "eye is on the sparrow" is also "watching me," touching and being touched, moving and being moved, by the "tragic beauty of life." God's providence inspires social activism. God feels the joy and pain and the world and works within our lives and history to inspire the dream of Shalom and energize the stride toward freedom. "God is an adventurer and those who would affirm their fraternity must follow in His train."[33]

Yet, behind every "yes" is a corresponding "no." Too often, as both Whitehead and Thurman recognize, our visions of God have reflected the worst versions of ourselves and have inspired coercion and violence rather than loving hospitality and inspiration. According to Thurman:

> The world is not finished yet; yet that men do worship god, yes; and they obey the gods they worship; but the gods they worship are unworthy gods...the tragedy of life is that persons become like the gods they worship. These are not atheists. Men become like the gods they worship. If they are bad persons, it means that they are worshipping bad gods.[34]

The personal God of the universe, the God who searches and knows us, is on the side of Shalom, love, and justice, and inspires people to "let justice roll down like waters and righteousness like an ever-flowing stream." (Amos 5:24)

Common Ground

While Whitehead the philosopher and Thurman the spiritual teacher personally encountered the Holy in their unique ways, broadly speaking they described a similar reality: a universe characterized by relationships, experience, value, creativity, possibility, and openness. A world in which God enters every moment of experience as the source of hope and creative transformation. For both Thurman and Whitehead, God is both transcendent and immanent and eternal and temporal. God guides history globally and personally and invites humankind to move beyond passivity and self-interest to common ground and world loyalty. Theolo-

---

33 Howard Thurman, *Deep is the Hunger* (Richmond, IN: Friends United Press, 1964), 121.

34 Howard Thurman, *Walking with God: The Sermon Series of Howard Thurman – Moral Struggle and the Prophets*. Edited by Peter Eisenstadt and Walter Earl Fluker (Maryknoll, NY: Orbis Books, 2020), 57.

gy, cosmology, and spirituality are not value neutral because the Creative Principle of the Universe is not value neutral. For Whitehead, the teleology of the universe is aimed at beauty and complexity of experience and this demands that we honor the value of creation in its various manifestations. For Thurman, God seeks common ground in human history based on God's vision of unity. God is on the side of the dispossessed and marginalized, despite the injustices perpetrated in the name of Jesus.

The universe and human life are God permeated and God inspired and when we awaken to God's presence in history and life, we embark on a holy adventure of promoting beauty and justice for our human companions and claiming our vocation as God's companions in healing the planet. All life is interdependent and God's providence is woven through every moment of experience aiming at the incarnation of God's Beloved Community in our human lives and the movements of history and the quest for justice.

Awakening to God's Growing Edge

As a child walking along Atlantic beaches, Howard Thurman felt like "all things, the sand, the sea, the stars, the night, were one lung through which all life breathed." I have a similar feeling when I walk on the beaches of Cape Cod, the East Coast of Maryland and Delaware, and the Pacific coast of Monterrey and Santa Cruz. I feel God's Breath whispering through the trees on my predawn walks in my Potomac, Maryland, neighborhood. The Breath of God, often identified with the Holy Spirit, flows through us, energizing, enlightening, and enlivening. We feel the spirit of God as we sing, "breathe on me breath of God, fill me with life anew." We are connected with all things. There is no "other." We are joined with a child in Appalachia, a parent in Sudan, a family traveling north from Guatemala, and the families in our own neighborhood. There is no friend or foe, just children of God, who breathe God's love with us.

In this exercise, find a quiet place to rest, and simply breathe. Breathe in the breath of God, breathe in the spirit of God's presence. Let the Lung of the Universe fill you and awaken you to your connection with every life form. Breathe in the deeper unity of life that transcends politics, nation, race, gender, sexuality, age, and every division we falsely created. Breathe in the beauty of earth and share that beauty as you exhale.

Throughout the day, let God breathe through you, especially when you become preoccupied with anxiety, busyness, or fearful thoughts. When you feel alienated from one of God's children, pause and breathe deeply, letting go of your fear and distance even as you challenge. Let your breath join you and empower you to be God's uniting and affirming presence. God's voice of peace and justice.

Every breath can be a prayer for unity and healing. Every breath can energize us to be instruments of God's peace. Breath on us breath of God. Fill us with life anew.

A Prayer from the Growing Edge

Thurman quotes this poem in *Deep is the Hunger,* as a prayer for the stature we need for the living of these days. We need spiritual stature and the ability to embrace otherness and contrast to inspire protest against injustice, sacrifice for the greater good, and empathy for both the vulnerable and powerful.

Each night my bonny, sturdy lad
 Persists in adding to his, Now I lay me
Down to sleep, the earnest wistful plea:
"God, make me big."
And I, his mother, with greater need,
Do echo in a humbled, contrite heart,"God, make me big."[35]

---

35 Howard Thurman, *Deep is the Hunger* (Richmond, IN: Friends United Press), 86

CHAPTER FOUR

JESUS: MYSTIC, MENTOR, AND MORAL GUIDE

When the Western world accepted Christianity, Caesar conquered...The brief Galilean vision of humility flickered throughout the ages, uncertainly. In the official formation of the religion, it has assumed the trivial form of the mere attribution of to the Jews that they cherished a misconception about their Messiah. But the deeper idolatry, of the fashioning of God in the image of the Egyptian, Persian, and Roman imperial rulers was retained. The Church gave unto God the attributes which belonged exclusively to Caesar.[1]

> His days were nurtured in great hostilities,
> Focused on his kind, the sons of Israel,
> There was no moment in all his years
> When he was free.[2]

Jesus is at the heart of Whitehead's and Thurman's vision of reality and social transformation. To speak of the centrality of Jesus in Thurman's life is obvious. He was raised in the evangelical Black Baptist tradition, where our personal relationship to Jesus

---

1 Alfred North Whitehead, *Process and Reality: The Corrected Edition*, edited by David Ray Griffin and Donald Sherburne (New York: Free Press, 1978), 343.

2 Howard Thurman, *Jesus and the Disinherited* (Boston: Beacon Press, 1996), 34.

could be a matter of heaven or hell, as he discovered at his father's funeral. Although Thurman transcended the conservative and doctrinal religion of his Baptist roots in favor of a universalist God revealed in every path toward truth and in the world's great religious leaders, Jesus was central to many of Thurman's writings, including his many meditations on Christmas as well as his book *Jesus and the Disinherited,* arguably the first African American liberation theology.

As the son and grandson of Anglican priests, mainstream Christianity was at heart of Whitehead's childhood and youth. Whitehead often went on church related visits with his father and grandfather and was tutored as a child and youth in the creeds and liturgies of the Christian church. It is likely that he knew the Nicene Creed by heart and repeated it weekly in worship and regularly recited the Christology of the Creed:

> We believe in one Lord, Jesus Christ, the only Son of God, eternally begotten of the Father, God from God, Light from Light, true God from true God, begotten, not made, of one Being with the Father; through him all things were made. For us and for our salvation he came down from heaven, was incarnate from the Holy Spirit and the Virgin Mary and was made man. For our sake he was crucified under Pontius Pilate; he suffered death and was buried. On the third day he rose again in accordance with the Scriptures; he ascended into heaven and is seated at the right hand of the Father. He will come again in glory to judge the living and the dead, and his kingdom will have no end.

No doubt he also regularly recited the Apostles Creed. His family was cosmopolitan and well-educated. They also affirmed the traditional articles of faith at worship.

> I believe in Jesus Christ,
> his only Son our Lord.
> He was conceived by the Holy Spirit
> and born of the Virgin Mary.

He suffered under Pontius Pilate,
was crucified, died, and was buried.
He descended to the dead.
On the third day he rose again.
He ascended into heaven,
and sits at the right hand of the Father.
From there he shall come again
to judge the living and the dead.

Although Whitehead questioned literal doctrinal understandings of God and Christ and was not an active church member
during his Harvard and Cambridge years, in many ways Whitehead's history of the evolution of Western philosophy and civilization is a hymn to the profound ethical and spiritual impact of
Jesus and Plato. The vision of God presented in the final chapter
in Whitehead's *Process and Reality* can be seen as a cosmological in-
terpretation of Whitehead's relational and responsive description
of the Galilean origins of Christianity.

In the following paragraphs, I will explore the meaning of
Jesus in Whitehead and Thurman. While their vision of Jesus or
Christ is non-creedal, the life of Jesus shaped their understanding
of God and God's purposes in the human and cosmic adventures.
Their vision of Jesus challenged the inherent violence and idolatry of authoritarian and unilateral images of God and their promotion of authoritarian and backward looking ecclesiastical and
political institutions.

Whitehead, Jesus, and the Power of Love

In contrast to many interpretations of Whitehead's philosophy, I accent the importance of Jesus as an inspiration and exemplar of Whitehead's philosophical vision. The world lives by the
incarnation of God and the life of Jesus can be understood as a
unique incarnation or reflection of divine immanence. Without
denying Whitehead's universalism, I believe that Whitehead's God
is the reflection writ large of his Galilean vision of Jesus. I believe

that Whitehead's theological vision answers the challenge he poses in *Religion in the Making:*

> Buddhism and Christianity find their origins respective-
> ly in two inspired moments of history: the life of Buddha, and
> the life of Christ. Buddha gave his doctrine to enlighten the
> world; Christ gave his life. It is for Christians to discern the
> doctrine.[3]

In many ways, Whitehead understands the life of Jesus as a revelation of God's power as persuasive and relational and not coercive and domineering. In that spirit, my Claremont teacher Bernard Loomer spoke of two kinds of power: relational, interdependent power which responds as well as creates and which seeks a democracy of creativity and revelation and the contrasting unilateral or authoritarian power, which creates but is not influenced by the world and seeks to limit freedom and confine religion to the narrow parameters of dogma. These two kinds of power can also be described in terms of the distinction between Jesus the revelation of the Galilean vision and Caesar the embodiment of the authoritarian vision, that is, the power of love and the love of power, respectively. According to Whitehead,

> the life of Christ is not an expedition of over-ruling pow-
> er...Its power lies in the absence of force. It has the deci-
> siveness of a supreme ideal, and that is why the history of
> the world divides at this point in time.[4]

In describing the evolution of Christianity, Whitehead asserts that "on the whole, the Gospel of Love was turned into the Gospel of Fear" and counsels that "if the modern world is to find God, it must find him through love and not fear, with the help of John and not of Paul."[5]

---

3   Whitehead, *Religion in the Making* (New York: Meridian, 1960) , 55.
4   Ibid,, 56-57.
5   Ibid. 72-73.

In contrast to the authoritarian Caesar, who rules by coercion and threat of punishment, the God of the Galilean vision, reflected in the life of Jesus, guides the world by God's vision of truth, beauty, and goodness, encouraging freedom and creativity. When Whitehead speaks of God as the "fellow sufferer who understands," his image of God is guided by the Galilean vision. God's power is grounded in God's empathy and connectedness with the world. "The power by which God sustains the world is the power of the ideal," incarnate in the aim toward the production of beauty as well as the inspiration to abandon self-interest in favor of world loyalty in our personal lives.[6]

Whitehead describes two critical moments in the evolution of Western philosophy, religion, and civilization, still yet to be realized as we witness the political demagoguery, violence, and authoritarianism of our time. The first moment, or phase, is found in Plato's affirmation "the divine element in the world is to be perceived as a persuasive agency and not as a coercive agency," which should be seen as "one of the greatest intellectual discoveries in the history of religion." Whitehead adds that "the second phase is the supreme moment in religious history, according to Christianity. The essence of Christianity is the appeal to the life of Christ and his agency in the world."[7]

Whitehead does not attempt a scholarly analysis of Jesus' life. Rather, in language bordering on poetry that inspires metaphysics as well as politics, Whitehead rhapsodizes:

> But there can be no doubt as to what elements in the [gospel] record have evoked a response from all that is best in human nature. The Mother, the Child, the bare manger: the lowly man, homeless and self-forgetful, with his message of peace, love, and sympathy: the suffering, the agony, the tender words as life ebbed, the final despair: the whole with the authority of supreme victory.

---

6   Whitehead, *Religion and the Making*, 149.
7   Whitehead, *Adventures of ideas* (New York: Free Press, 1933), 166-167.

I need not elaborate. Can there be any doubt that the power of Christianity lies in its revelation in act, of that which Plato divined in theory?[8]

While Whitehead does not develop a theory of social transformation and activism, the seeds of a relationally oriented politics are found in Whitehead's vision of Jesus, writ large in the philosopher's vision of God's relationship to the world. Social change seeks to be in harmony with the teleology of the universe and its aim at the production of beauty and must, accordingly, aim at the formation of institutions that promote the production of beauty and the establishment of peace in human relationships and society. This involves joining both the means and the ends in such a way that the value and voices of others are affirmed and recognized. While all political power, even that exercised in positive and liberating social change, virtually always involves an element of coercion, the goal of relational political power is to seek the "more perfect union" by persuasion rather than coercion. In Whitehead's estimation, Jesus and Buddha reflect universal values that can be embodied in daily life and political decision-making. These values include the honoring of diversity, the universality of revelation and value, and the privileging of persuasion over coercion and relationship over authoritarianism. Jesus' persuasive vision reflects the universality of God's concern for the well-being of humankind and creation, and thus seeks to include everyone in the Beloved Community.

Whitehead's affirmation that the world lives by the incarnation of God is personal as well as global in nature. God's presence in the world is universal and intimate: to exist is to be touched by God even if we choose to go against God's vision for our lives. No one, not even the white nationalist, Hamas insurrectionist, Israeli soldier, or liberative theologian, is excluded from God's inspiration and all should be part of our quest, to quote Thurman, for a friendly world of friendly people. God's incarnation is evident in each creature's quest for abundant life – to live, to live well, and

8   Ibid., 167.

to live better – and in the highest wisdom of the world's great religious and philosophical traditions. In the life of Jesus, as well as that of Buddha, Whitehead sees the inspiration for the peace that passes all understanding, the movement from self-interest to world loyalty in which our well-being is identified with the well-being of the whole. Christ's persuasive love inspires a democracy of the spirit, the recognition that value and experience are universal, which encourages the practice of democratic and inclusive, rather than demagogic and authoritarian, forms of community and political decision-making. Any creature touched by God, and any human being reflecting God's presence, regardless of race, nation of origin, or sexual identity, possesses value, deserves our ethical consideration, and requires a role in determining the communities of which they are residents.

Thurman's Liberating Jesus

Twenty-seven hundred years ago, the Greek philosopher Xenophanes of Colophon (570-478 BCE) challenged his contemporaries' anthropomorphic images of God as far too human in their jealousies and foibles and not suitable for the moral and spiritual advancement of humankind.

> If cattle or horses or lions had hands and could draw,
> And could sculpt like men,
>   then the horses would draw their gods
> Like horses, and cattle like cattle; and each would shape
> Bodies of gods in the likeness, each kind, of their own.

In his classic *The Quest for the Historical Jesus*, pioneering New Testament scholar Albert Schweitzer came to a similar conclusion. Schweitzer believed that as earnest and articulate as Biblical scholars were in their quest to find historical clues to the real Jesus beneath the creeds and myths, the Jesus they unearthed, was often a mirror for their theological orientation.

Whitehead and Thurman would affirm Schweitzer's insights in our understanding of the ultimate realities of our lives. On the one hand, it is tempting, despite God's universal revelation, either consciously or unconsciously, to form a God in our image, a God who "looks *only* like me," and reflects our own political, economic, ethnic, and theological prejudices. All politics is local, as former Speaker of the House Tip O'Neill noted, and it is impossible to completely transcend our social, political, gender, and economic location. We need to be honest in our recognition that every vision of God and Jesus, even those that arise out of mystical experiences, reflects our perspective, place, and time. This is natural and appropriate, given the nature of incarnational love is to be "one of us," as singer Joan Osborne chants. Still, we also need to be clear that none of our images of God fully encompass God's nature and that some images of God and Jesus can cure, while others can kill. Jesus can become the intentional or unintentional tool of our quest for power and domination. Jesus can also be the inspiration for adventure and liberation. To reiterate an earlier quote from Thurman:

> The world is not finished yet; yet that men do worship god, yes; and they obey the gods they worship; but the gods they worship are unworthy gods…the tragedy of life is that persons become like the gods they worship. These are not atheists. Men become like the gods they worship. If they are bad persons, it means that they are worshipping bad gods.[9]

Theological reflection and religious practice are ambiguous, according to both Thurman and Whitehead. Our images of God, and of Jesus, can inspire us to march onward as Christian soldiers going "as to war" armed with the cross of Jesus or live by Jesus' affirmation, "blessed are the peacemakers."

In recent years, critics of theology and scripture, within and beyond Christianity, have recognized that the Jesus of the Gospels

9   Howard Thurman, *Walking with God: The Sermon Series of Howard Thurman – Moral Struggle and the Prophets.* Edited by Peter Eisenstadt and Walter Earl Fluker (Maryknoll, NY: Orbis Books, 2020), 57.

has been domesticated and described in ways that fit into – and encourage - the Western world's individualism, economics, and sovereign responsibility for lesser races, based on our perception of European cultural and religious superiority, to civilize the "benighted" worlds of Asia, Africa, and the Americas through colonization and eradication of indigenous traditions. The Radical Reformers and parents of the Mennonite tradition, looking even further back in Christian history, asserted that the Fall of Christianity occurred when the Roman sovereign Constantine (272-337) marched into Rome flying the Christian flag and substituted institutional power and privilege, and monolithic doctrine and church leadership, for the simple, compassionate, and egalitarian message of Jesus.

Thurman and Whitehead both lamented the identification of Christianity with religious and political institutionalism and its quest for uniformity, control, power, and the maintenance of the status quo. Reflecting on his own experience in Jim Crow South as well as listening to Grandmother Nancy Ambrose's stories of slavery, Thurman recognized the ambiguities of Christian faith: Christianity could be the basis for racism and violence toward persons of color; and the message of Jesus could also be the catalyst of liberation. Thurman would concur with Whitehead's assertion that God must be found through love and not fear, through the vision of John and not that of Paul. Thurman recalled his grandmother's refusal to have him read the epistles of Paul as a result of her regularly hearing slave masters invoke the apostle's counsel "slaves, obey your masters" (Ephesians 6:5-9). His grandmother wisely recognized the difference between the liberating Jesus of the Gospels and the stifling proponent of institutional Christianity's unjust and coercive status quo. She knew in her cells as well as her soul the radical difference between the power of love and the love of power, the power that affirms and liberates and the power that subjugates and destroys.

Thurman was a harsh critique of institutional and dogmatic Christianity and the attempt to make Jesus the bastion of unjust social structures. Thurman felt no need to defend Christianity from its critics, whether they were challenging his Christian faith as an African American during his several month journey through India sponsored by the YWCA or from North American activists and intellectuals who saw Christianity as a hindrance to the stride toward freedom.

Thurman clearly distinguished the wide chasm between institutional and political Christianity and the faith of Jesus of Nazareth. Although mild mannered and seldom prone to hyperbole in his denunciation of North American Christianity, Thurman's mystical experience of the Holy was always understood in light of his experience as a Black man in a society that judged him as inferior, threatening, and in need of the control and tutelage of his white superiors. On more than one occasion, Thurman noted that outsiders' critiques of Christianity could never be as harsh as his own. Outsiders viewed the cooption of Jesus by racist, capitalist, and authoritarian perspectives; Thurman felt this manipulation and idolatry of Christian racism in his cells, bones, and in his access to the levers of respect and power. Thurman rebelled rightly against any form of binary political or religious separatism, which denied the value and humanity of persons outside our religious or racial community or circle of concern. Thurman believed that Christianity is doomed to become an irrelevant religious movement unless it disengages itself from and offers a healing alternative to white supremacy. Thurman would have recognized the well documented de-evangelizing impact of white Christian nationalism and "evangelical" loyalty to Donald Trump over the way of Jesus.

Thurman begins his classic *Jesus and the Disinherited*, perhaps the first Black liberation theology, published initially in 1949, with the affirmation: "the significance of Jesus for people who stand with their backs against the wall has seemed to me to be crucial... the interest in the problem has been and continues to be both personal and professional." Thurman asks the probing question, "Why is it that Christianity seems impotent to deal radically, and therefore effectively, with the issues of discrimination and injustice on the basis of race, religion, and national origin? Is this impotency due to a betrayal of the genius of the religion, or is it due to a basic weakness in the religion itself?"[10]

Thurman's quest to understand the message of Jesus is aimed at providing a vision of wholeness and liberation "for those who stand, at a moment in human history, with their backs against the wall."[11] According to Thurman, we cannot discuss Jesus life and work from sidelines. How we articulate Jesus' life and message can be a matter of life or death, and freedom or control, for marginalized and oppressed people. Jesus means freedom and the freedom found in Jesus must be experienced in Common Ground, Thurman's term for what Martin Luther King, following the philosopher Josiah Royce, described as the Beloved Community. Jesus is a concrete person who lived in space and time, was embedded in the history of his people and shaped by the machinations of Empire, and yet rose above with a message of liberation for all humankind. Thurman notes an irony in the history of Christianity:

> Too often the price exacted by society for security is that the Christian movement in its formal expression must be on the side of the strong against the weak. This is a matter of tremendous significance, for it reveals to what extent a religion that was born of a people acquainted with persecution and suffering has become the cornerstone of a civilization and nations whose very position in modern life has been secured a ruthless use of power applied to weak and defenseless peoples.[12]

Lest we think that Thurman's words have been rendered archaic by Civil Rights legislation and the election of an African American President and Indian and African American (of Jamaican descent) Vice-President, we need only look at the rise of white Christian nationalism, invectives by "Christian" politicians

---

10 Howard Thurman, *Jesus and the Disinherited* (Boston: Beacon Press, 1996), xix.

11 Ibid., 1.

12 Ibid., 2.

against immigrants and asylum seekers describing them as vermin, thugs, rapists, and barely human, and the waving of a $60 Bible, cobbled together with the Constitution, Pledge of Allegiance, and Declaration of Independence, by a politician who seldom darkens a church door, models the seven deadly sins without remorse, and whose behavior and politics are intended to inspire the worst angels of human nature and whose most ardent supporters see themselves as the orthodox Christian defenders of the faith against pluralism, diversity, racial equality, and the impact of human creativity. Tragically, the identification of Christianity with racism, demagoguery, and misogyny existed long before Donald Trump and will likely continue long after he's left the scene of national politics.

Jesus is at the heart of Thurman's politics, mysticism, and theological vision. For Thuman, Jesus is the Great Companion and Friend. Thurman's understanding of Jesus was personal and experiential rather than creedal. Thurman notes that more than any theologian or theological school, his grandmother Nancy Ambrose, a former slave who never learned to read revealed him the personality of Jesus. Thurman testifies:

> I learned more, for instance, about the genius of the religion of Jesus from my grandmother than from all the men who taught me...Greek and all the rest of it. Because she moved inside the experience and lived out of that kind of center.[13]

Jesus is the approachable revelation of a God to whom we can confide our fears and aspirations and who guides our ethical and political decision-making. Thurman's God is Jesus-like and Jesus represents God's love for the world in all its wondrous diversity and tragic beauty. As I reflected on Thurman's vision of Jesus, I was reminded of the intimacy of God described in two songs from my Baptist childhood, "In the Garden" and "What a Friend We Have in Jesus." While Thurman may not have sung "In the Garden" as

---

13   Luther E. Smith, Jr., *Howard Thurman: The Mystic as Prophet, 39.*

child given the date of its composition in 1913, "What a Friend
We Have in Jesus," a poem set to music in 1868, would likely have
been part of Thurman's religious upbringing due to its popularity
in evangelical Baptist circles. When we walk "in the garden" in
moments of solitude, Jesus is as near to us as he was to Mary of
Magdala who heard Jesus calling her name on Easter morning:

> And He walks with me, and He talks with me,
> And He tells me I am His own,
> And the joy we share as we tarry there,
> None other has ever known.

Broken by injustice and racism, we discover that there is a
"balm in Gilead," when we hear Jesus calling our name. Even if
others disparage and diminish us, Jesus addresses us by name as
son, daughter, and friend, and claims us as his beloved companion, something more powerful and transformative than any racist
chant.

I can imagine Thurman relating his experience of speaking
with Jesus under the big oak tree to the sentiments of "What a
Friend We Have in Jesus":

> What a friend we have in Jesus,
> All our sins and griefs to bear!
> What a privilege to carry
> Everything to God in prayer!
> Oh, what peace we often forfeit,
> Oh, what needless pain we bear,
> All because we do not carry
> Everything to God in prayer![14]

Yet, the Jesus of Thurman's theology was a far cry from the
sentimental, individualistic "Jesus and me" theology of much
white evangelical Christianity. Thurman believes that the Jesus of
popular Christianity has been sanitized, domesticated, and rendered harmless and ahistorical and thus irrelevant to our current

---

14 Lyrics by Joseph M. Scriven, 1855.

unjust social situation. Worse yet, Jesus has been used to further racism, injustice, and unbridled capitalism. The Jesus of the Gospels, the authentic Jesus, to whom we can confide in prayer, is the companion and liberator of the marginalized, oppressed, and forgotten and not the mascot of the powerful and prosperous. Jesus had a backbone and a message to the downtrodden that drowned out the oppressors' falsehood: "you are my beloved, you are the light of the world, you are my son, my daughter, and my companion, and you deserve to be free. Glory Hallelujah!"

In *Jesus and the Disinherited,* Thurman alerts his readers to the often-forgotten realities of Jesus' life, omitted in popular evangelical and conservative white Christian understandings of Jesus as arbiter of the status quo and enemy of social transformation:

Jesus was a Jew, a member of a community with a strong religious heritage and history, grounded in the covenantal relationship of God and the Jewish people.

Jesus was a member of an oppressed community and never was able to forge his personal political destiny.

Jesus poor, a member of the hard-working peasant class, often living from day to day and week to week.

Jesus was fully human not only in his realization of the highest human aspirations but also his total embeddedness in the natural order of things. Fully human, Jesus was fully natural, and was not the result of a supernatural act of God nor did Jesus violate the laws of nature in his ministry. There is a continuity of experience that joins Jesus and us.

Jesus was also fully divine, although his divinity was grounded in his humanity and continuity with us. As Luther Smith notes, "there was no more God incarnate in Jesus than any other man or woman. Jesus had a greater consciousness of God and relationship to, his divinity. This was a result of Jesus working at a closer relatedness with God."[15] Jesus was the exemplar of what is possible for human life. Looking at Jesus' life naturalistically, we can

---

15 Luther E. Smith, Jr. *Howard Thurman: Mystic and Prophet,* 62-63. I am grateful for Smith's insights on Thurman's vision of Jesus.

understand the early Christian affirmation, "God became human that humans might become divine" in ways that empower us to do "greater things" than we can imagine as followers and companions of Jesus.

For Thurman, Jesus is the vision of hope and inspiration for protest for the oppressed and marginalized. While Jesus' liberating message can heal the apathy and hard-heartedness of the powerful and wealthy, Jesus our Companion, Challenger, and Friend speaks most intimately with those whose backs are against the wall. In words that speak to the twenty-first as well as first centuries:

> The striking similarity between the social position of Jesus in Palestine and the vast majority of African Negroes is obvious to anyone who tarries long over the facts.[16]

Let your imagination enter the experience of Jesus and oppressed people everywhere as you meditate on Thurman's words:

> Now Jesus was not a Roman citizen. He was not protected by the normal guarantees of citizenship – that quiet sense of security that comes from knowing that you belong and the general climate of confidence that it inspires. If a Roman soldier pushed Jesus into a ditch, he could not appeal to Caesar; he would just be another Jew in the ditch…What stark insecurity.[17]

Now consider these words, written in the late 1940's, but relevant to the current experience of many African Americans in the United States, not to mention undocumented workers, and persons in Gaza, West Bank, Sudan, and Ukraine today. "The Negro has felt with some justification, that the police officer of the community provides no defense against the offending or offensive white man. Thus the Negro feels that he must be prepared, at a moment's notice, to protect his own life and take the consequence therefor."[18]

---

16   Thurman, *Jesus and the Disinherited,* 23.
17   Ibid., 23.
18   Ibid., 24.

In this dire situation, without political power, Jesus proclaimed that survival of the whole person depended on cultivating
their inner life. Regardless of circumstances, you are God's beloved
child. God's eye is on the sparrow and God is watching you. Moreover, you can experience Jesus as the voice of peace, healing, and
courage in the challenges of life. Jesus described a world in which
"there would be room for all, and no man would be a threat to his
brother. 'The kingdom of God is within.' 'The Spirit of the Lord
is upon me to preach the Gospel to the poor.'"[19] To the marginalized and downtrodden throughout the ages, Jesus remains an image and inspiration to hope, protest, and creativity. Jesus energizes
prayerful protest which liberates oppressor and oppressed alike.

> The birth of Jesus remains the symbol of the dignity and
> inherent worthfulness of the common man…Jesus Christ was
> born in a stable, he was born of humble surroundings that are
> the common lot of those who earn their living by the sweat of
> their brows. Nothing can rob the common man of this heri-
> tage – when he beholds Jesus he sees in him the possibilities
> of life even for the humblest and a dramatic resolution of the
> meaning of God.[20]

For Thurman, the greatest possibility emerging from Jesus'
ministry is his affirmation of each person as God's beloved child,
infinite in value, as the foundation for the Peaceable Realm, the
Common Ground, the Beloved Community. In Jesus' all-embracing love for tax collectors, unclean persons, Roman soldiers, and
religious zealots, we discover that "every man is potentially every
other man's neighbor…a man must love his neighbor, directly,
clearly, with no barriers between."[21]   In loving the marginalized
and outcast, Jesus enabled them to love themselves and claim their
voices as agents of their personal and ethnic destiny. Jesus liberates
people of all economic classes and ethnicities from fear and hate
by enabling us to recognize our true dignity as God's beloved chil-

19   Ibid., 24.
20   Howard Thurman, *The Mood of Christmas*, 11.
21   Thurman, *Jesus and the Disinherited*, 79.

dren and to see God's love embracing rich and poor and powerful and powerless alike.

Jesus' death on the Cross was an act of loving devotion to his mission, and not a sacrifice to appease a wrathful and angry God. Jesus' death was not predestined to free us from the impact of original sin but the result of the violence institutional evil. Beyond the Cross is the Resurrection, which reveals that "the greatest discovery we can make concerning Jesus is that, at long last, death could not touch in him that which gave to his life its great significance."[22] Jesus' message lives on in the quest for salvation that encompasses body, mind, spirit, and relationships, as well as moral and spiritual arcs of history. As a bumper sticker placards, "If you love Jesus, seek justice. Any fool can honk!" To follow Jesus is to seek abundant life for all God's children, regardless of their ethnicity, sexual identity, nation of origin, or citizenship status.

Common Ground

Although Whitehead and Thurman came from vastly different social, economic, and racial locations, they shared the vision of Jesus and Christianity at its best as a catalyst for freedom and self-affirmation and protest against injustice and dehumanization. For Thurman, Jesus taught the infinite value of human personality. As God's beloved children, we matter and our value before God must be realized individually and politically in the quest for Common Ground or Beloved Community. For Whitehead, value is universal and to deface the value of any creature is to go against the grain of the universe. The current of the universe, the teleology of the universe incarnate in Jesus' life, as Whitehead states, is aimed at the production of beauty. The realization of beauty in human life results from the intentional creation of structures of beauty that inspire and facilitate greatness of experience not only for the "elite" but also for the "everyday" person. The spirit that inspired Jesus to preach good news to the poor is universal in

---

22 Thurman, *Deep is the Hunger,* 177.

nature and echoes through history inspiring a divine restlessness in our hearts and reminding us always to keep our eyes on the prize of Shalom. The pure conservative, as Whitehead says, goes against the grain of the universe, whether in education, religion, economics, foreign policy, and politics. The God of the Growing Edge calls us forward to new horizons in which all God's children "walk hand in hand."

Thurman's God of the Growing Edge and Whitehead's Eros of Adventure, incarnate in Jesus the mystic, healer, and prophet, who is present in every quest for truth and every challenge to the idolatry of privilege and power. God inspires each creature and the varied religious traditions of the world are expressions of Divine Inspiration and not a fall from grace. Wherever truth and beauty are found, in sanctuary, mosque, ashram, or sweat lodge, God is present as its inspiration and God wants us to promote beauty of experience for all God's children.

Although neither Whitehead nor Thurman penned a theology of world religions, their vision of God's love and revelation is the basis for interfaith community. Long before the phrase "multiple belonging" was coined to describe a person's integration of practices from a variety of faith traditions, Whitehead asserted that the flourishing of Buddhism and Christianity in the modern world required their mutual affirmation and embrace of each other's truths. Thurman employed the scriptures and symbols of other faith traditions in the course of his religious and university community's worship services. People of other faiths found a spiritual home at Boston University's Marsh Chapel and the Church of the Fellowship of All Peoples. Thurman believed that truth is found in every authentic human path. The quest for justice and equality involves the commitment of the world's religious communities to go beyond their own parochialism to join together as companions to further the global Beloved Community.

Awakening to God's Growing Edge

Thurman was known for his imaginative approach to worship and spiritual formation. He was committed to helping his congregants and those who sought his spiritual guidance experience the living truths of faith rather than merely the lifeless words of doctrine. For Thurman, as well as Whitehead, religious traditions have their origin in the experience of remarkable spirit persons, to use the language of Marcus Borg, who have direct experience of the Holy and communicate their experience of the Holy to others. Think of Moses' encounter with the burning bush, Jacob's ladder of angels, Buddha under the Bo Tree, Jesus in the wilderness and on the cross, Mary of Magdala in the Garden, and Mohammed in the cave. In the spirit of Mary Oliver's poem, they paid attention, were amazed, and told about their experiences in ways that opened others to the Divine.

St. Benedict of Nursia taught a practice of encountering scripture and other holy texts that today we identify as Lectio Divina or holy reading. The point of holy reading is to personalize the scripture moving from the words to the Living Word of mystical encounter available to each one of us. The steps of a contemporary version of Lectio Divina are as follows:

A time of stillness.

Prayer of openness and gratitude

Reading the scripture twice with a time of stillness between readings.

Silent openness to the message of the scripture, the word or phrase, hymn or image, that is addressed to you.

In a time of silence, you may choose to sit in a comfortable chair or you might go for a walk and simply let your mind wander until an inspiration emerges.

Reflect on the meaning of the word for you at this point in your life.

Jot down some notes as a way of grounding and preserving your experience.

The practice of holy reading initially had its primary use in discerning the deeper personal meaning of scripture. You can, however, use this practice for any media – a poem, quote, or even a painting or piece of music.

I often use the practice of holy reading to gain insights for my sermon and lecture preparation. I also use it to discern the deeper meaning of a text I'm writing. For example, in the writing of this text, I took a walk with Jesus as my companion after taking notes for this chapter. I had "just a little talk with Jesus" as I asked for guidance as to what words God would speak to me about the role of Jesus in Whitehead and Thurman and how I might best express their understandings of Jesus to you, my readers. As I walked along, I had the insight that "Jesus is a significant influence on Whitehead's metaphysical vision" and that Whitehead's understanding of God as creative-responsive love can be understood as a reflection of Jesus' relational ministry. In living with the wisdom of Whitehead and Thurman, my goal was to experience a spiritual connection to the texts, an insight or intuition, and not just an analysis. In so doing, my words would come from heart as well as mind, and spirit as well as intellect, joining them in a holistic vision which joined my spirit with the spirits of Thurman and Whitehead. This chapter is the fruit of this unexpected insight.

In your practice of holy reading, I invite you to listen prayerfully and imaginatively to the following text, listening for God's Word in the words of the text as it applies to your life. Read contemplatively the Gospel of Mark's account of Jesus' encounter with a woman from another ethnic group (Mark 7:24-30).

> Now Jesus got up and went from there to the region of Tyre. And when He had entered a house, He wanted no one to know *about it*; and *yet* He could not escape notice. But after hearing about Him, a woman whose little daughter had an unclean spirit immediately came and fell at His feet. Now the woman was a Gentile, of Syrophoenician descent. And she *repeatedly* asked Him to cast the demon out of her daughter. And He was saying to her, "Let the children be satisfied

first, for it is not good to take the children's bread and throw it to the dogs." But she answered and said to Him, "Yes, Lord, *but* even the dogs under the table feed on the children's crumbs." And He said to her, "Because of this answer, go; the demon has gone out of your daughter." And after going back to her home, she found the child lying on the bed, and the demon gone.

In response to reading this challenging scripture twice prayerfully and meditatively:

  1) What words, images, or memories, etc. emerge?
  2) In what ways are you complicit in creating outsiders?
  3) What is their meaning for your life today,
  4) How might you embody this inspiration in daily life?

Conclude with a prayer of gratitude as you ask, seek, and knock for inspiration in incarnating the Word of God in the words of scripture.

A Prayer from the Growing Edge

Thurman saw Jesus as an image of hope and liberation for those whose backs are against the wall. Whether privileged or powerless, we need to shine light in the chaos of incivility, prejudice, hatred, violence, and disinformation. Light guides our path and restores our hope and courage to transform the world.

I will light candles of joy, despite all sadness.
Candles of hope, where despair keeps watch.
Candles of Courage for fears everpresent,
Candles of peace for tempest tossed days,
Candles of grace to ease heavy burdens,
Candles of love to inspire all my living,
Candles that will burn all year long.[23]

---

23 Howard Thurman, *The Meaning of Christmas, 19.*

CHAPTER FIVE

SPIRITUALITY AND SOCIAL TRANSFORMATION

The worship of God is not a rule of safety—it is an adventure of the spirit, a flight after the unattainable. The death of religion comes with the repression of the high hope of adventure.[1]

For the mystic, social action is sacramental, because it is not an end in itself. Always, it is the individual who must be addressed, located and released, underneath his misery and his hunger and his destitution. That whatever may be blocking his way to his own center where his altar may be found, this must be removed."[2]

Worship is unsafe, it could inspire you to take an adventure of the spirit and challenge the mores of your social order. Social action is sacramental, it awakens us to the Heart of the World present in all creation, waiting to be liberated. Worship may be especially unsafe to those who want to cling to power and connect their prosperity with the poverty and powerlessness of others. Those who protest injustice must also take risks: the risk of conflict and unpopularity, sometimes the risk of reputation and life, and the risk of seeing the holiness of those whose

1   Alfred North Whitehead, *Science and the Modern World* (New York: Free Press, 1967), 192.

2   *Mysticism and Social Action: Lawrence Lectures and Discussions with Howard Thurman (*London: LARF, 2014), Kindle location, 249-251.

behaviors they challenge. We must also take the risk of embracing change ourselves, and jettisoning familiar but limiting visions to embrace novel and spacious visions and alternative possibilities.

Although neither Thurman nor Whitehead claimed the title theologian as their primary vocational title, both recognized the relationship between our images of God, spiritual experiences, and ethical and political commitments. Both changed the face of modern theology. Whitehead gave voice to a new vision of God defined by relationality and partnership and inspired the emergence of the process and open and relational theology movements. Whitehead's metaphysical vision inspired what may be the first full length theological text dealing with the ecological crisis, my professor John Cobb's *Is It Too Late?* Thurman was described as the "schoolmaster" of the Civil Rights movement in his affirmation of the unity of spirituality, non-violence, and social change. During the height of the Civil Rights movement, Thurman's *Jesus and the Disinherited* was Martin Luther King's constant companion, tucked away in his briefcase.

Whitehead asserted that a person's "character is formed according to your faith." Moreover, "a religion, on its doctrinal side, can thus be described as a system of general truths which has the effect of transforming character when they are sincerely held and vividly apprehended."[3] Whitehead noted that religion is not always beneficial; it can stifle creativity, persecute innovation, privilege the status quo, and promote authoritarian and coercive political and ecclesiastical institutions.

Thurman recognized the power of theological doctrines to heal or harm. He knew first-hand the theologies of oppression and domination that separated humans by race, defining one race as superior, others as inferior and, thus, undeserving of basic human rights. Remembering the hellfire and brimstone sermon at his father's funeral, Thurman knew first-hand the soul-deadening power of unimaginative and exclusivist orthodoxy. Thurman, along with Whitehead, knew that some images of God could be demonic in

---

3   Whitehead, *Religion in the Making*, 15.

their brutality, coercion, and exclusion. Thuman also recognized the liberating power of theology, revealed in the sermons of slave preachers, who proclaimed, based on their perception of God's image in every person, that slaves were God's children, deserving of freedom and justice, despite the abusive and soul-destroying theology of slave owners. Both Whitehead and Thurman saw God's revelation as universal, promoting the affirmation of human rights and democracy. In the democracy of revelation, there is no "other" or inferior nor is any culture or religion bereft of divine inspiration. In God's realm, there are no "aliens," whether "undocumented" or of different races or sexual identities. God's realm has "many mansions" and God guides every path to truth and healing wherever it is found. God wants us, accordingly, to honor the wondrous diversity of humankind and all creation.

Grounded in God's universal love and revelation and God's valuing of all as God's beloved children, everyone has the right to abundant living, and every person has the responsibility to promote the well-being and self-actualization of their neighbor, regardless of race, gender, sexuality, nation of origin, religion, and age. Following the Logos theologians of the early Christian movement, Thurman and Whitehead believed that wherever truth is found, God is its source, whether in a laboratory, archeological dig, ashram, or mosque. "The true light, which enlightens everyone, was coming into the world." (John 1:9) I would add, in the context of the Christian mystical tradition, *Ubi caritas est vera, Deus ibi est,* where there is true charity, in whatever community or type of relationship it is found, God is present. True charity, or love, relates to our communities and social structures as well as individual relationships.

Whitehead was a child of the British privileged class, who supported the full admission of women and the children of working-class parents to university education and was an advocate of women's suffrage. Thurman pioneered black liberation, both as a mentor of a generation of Civil Rights leaders and as the author of the first full length book on black liberation, *Jesus and the*

Disinherited. Both saw God as a force for social change and the expansion of equality to embrace all persons. While Whitehead and Thurman did not directly address current issues such as climate change, LGBTQ+ rights, and reproductive rights, I believe that their visions of God's relational love and universal revelation can provide important insights in today's political and ethical decision-making.

Whitehead and Thurman are spiritual and theological guides for the ages and this very moment. Although their wisdom is timeless, they also recognized that theology and spirituality are embedded in the concreteness of everyday personal, economic, and political life. Grand visions must touch the ground of concrete experience or they have little value for people's lives. God is embedded in history and the motive force of the adventure of ideas and the promotion of social justice and beauty of experience. Accordingly, I must testify that this text also seeks to join the Infinite and the finite, the Global and local, and the Everlasting and the perpetual perishing. Accordingly, my reflections in this chapter are written in the backdrop of the ongoing Russian invasion of Ukraine; the Israel-Gaza conflict and the atrocities committed by both sides; student protests at universities across the globe; the rise of white nationalism among Christians; the polarization of political viewpoints and normalization incivility of American society; the demonization and threat of mass deportation of undocumented residents and the separation of families; the attack on the status of pastors and congregations who dare criticize the President; and the global reality of climate change (and climate change denial powered by "bible-believing" Christians) evident in forest fires, drought, storm, endangered species, sustained heat waves, and rising sea waters. The ambiguity of religion, especially Christianity in the USA, is obvious as many Christians align themselves with white nationalism, climate denial, denial of human rights, and anti-democratic policies. Intended to be a catalyst for freedom, Christianity has often been a taillight instead of a headlight, as

Martin Luther King noted, in furthering God's realm of Shalom, God's realm "on earth as it is in heaven."

As noted throughout this text, both Whitehead and Thurman were critical of religious institutions, recognizing that religion can purify the spirit, inspire mysticism, and further the moral and spiritual arcs of history. Religion can also be a vehicle of hate and oppression and provide the theological justification of racism, sexism, and violence against persons of other faith traditions and sexual identities. Inflexible and static doctrines, separating the faithful from outsiders, not only stifle the religious adventure but create a binary world of insiders and outsiders, saved and unsaved, and chosen and overlooked, that justifies violence, exclusion, domination, and injustice toward those outside the circle of salvation. To reiterate Thurman's quote from the previous chapter, "bad" gods lead to bad personal and political behaviors and these bad behaviors are often justified by privileging "bad" authoritarian, binary, and violent gods and their political and religious representatives.

Whitehead laments institutional Christianity's eclipsing the Galilean vision of Jesus with its focus on the power of love and prophetic persuasion to transform the world with the image of God as an all-determining Sovereign in the image of Caesar and its lust for power and domination. The quest for power leads to excommunication, heresy hunting, and violence to those who question the theological and political authorities ordained by the omnipotent Potentate. Authoritarian religion inspires authoritarian politics whether in the Holy Roman Empire, Muslim fundamentalism, 1930's Germany, Zionism, and the diabolical marriage of conservative Christianity, Trumpism, and white nationalism.

Thurman critiques institutional Christianity's eclipse of the prophetic Jesus' message of justice and inclusion by images of God as the guarantor of the status quo and the privileges of the wealthy and powerful. The faith that was born of healing, liberation, and hospitality, was abandoned for domination, colonialism, wealth, and servitude. For both Whitehead and Thurman, the future of faith requires choosing love over power and justice over privilege.

In Chapter Three, I described Whitehead's and Thurman's world views with attention to the relationship of theology, spirituality, and social transformation. In this chapter, I will go into greater detail in terms of the relationship of spirituality and social change, building on the insights of previous chapters. Mysticism leads to mission. Authentic spirituality leads to social transformation.

Whitehead's Politics of Beauty

Whitehead recognized the transformative power of mysticism in shaping history and cosmology, Whitehead affirmed the mystical roots of metaphysics. Accordingly, Whitehead notes "if you like to phrase it so, philosophy is mystical. For mysticism is direct insight into depths as yet unspoken."[4] Although Whitehead never wrote at any length about the mystic's calling, in response to the question "Shall we transcend our limitations?" in the course of a dialogue sponsored by the Cambridge Conversation Society, the Apostles, Whitehead responded, "I want to see God." Indeed, Whitehead's metaphysics reveals the significance of God in the unfolding of the universe, personal growth, and the quest for a truly adventurous and just civilization. Those who embrace Whitehead's vision personally will experience God in all things and all things in God. They will "see God" in flora and fauna, human diversity, and their own experiences.

Whitehead asserts that "the teleology of the universe is aimed at the production of Beauty" and that "any system of things which is in any wide sense beautiful is that extent justified in its existence."[5] The evolution of the universe as well as human evolution aims at the creation of environments that promote the complexity, intensity, and harmony of experience, characteristic of the realization of beauty in the lives of persons and institutions. Religious

---

4   Alfred North Whitehead, *Modes of Thought,* New York: Free Press, 1968), 174

5   Whitehead, *Adventures of Ideas,* 265

experience and theological reflection can, at their best, be factors in the realization of God's vision of human possibility "on earth as it is in heaven." The moral and spiritual arcs of the universe aim toward beauty in this moment of experience and over the long haul of history and their realization in our lives and the social order requires the integration of faith and practice. Yet, these moral and spiritual arcs cannot be significantly embodied in history without our commitment and effort, our willingness to embrace world loyalty, and claim our vocation as God's companions in healing the earth. In the following paragraphs, I will describe the impact of Whitehead's metaphysical vision on the quest for positive social transformation, the truly beautiful civilization.

The Divine Eros. Whitehead identifies God as Erotic or Passionate in nature. God never stands still, nor is God content with the world as it is. God aims at the experience of Beauty despite the tragedies of history. God has a vision and passion to embody the vision of truth, beauty, and goodness in the evolution of the universe and human civilization. Each moment reflects God's aim for intensity and complexity of experience and the seeds of Beauty for the future community as well as the individual in this present moment and over their lifespan. God is never on the sidelines but in the middle of life as source of possibilities for each moment and the long haul of history. The Infinite is the intimate companion present in every moment of experience and our life span.

> [God's] purpose is always embodied in the particular ideals relevant to the actual state of the world. Thus all attainment is immortal in that it fashions the actual ideas which are God in the world as it is now. Every act leaves the world with a deeper or fainter impress of God. He then passes into his next relation to the world with enlarged, or diminished, presentation of ideal values.[6]

God, the Divine Eros of the Universe, is the origin of the prophetic restlessness that reveals the distance between our current

---

6   Whitehead, *Religion in the Making,* 152.

personal and social structure and what could be in God's realm of Shalom. The ultimate source of the order of the universe, God is also the primary challenger to the status quo. The 8th century BCE prophet Amos experiences God's dream for the world and seeks to embody the Divine dream in the lives of the Northern Kingdom of Israel:

> Let justice roll down like water
>   and righteousness like an ever-flowing stream.
> (Amos 5:24)

God inspires the laughter of children, the devotion of scientists and parents, the creativity of poets and musicians, and the protest of prophets. God is the inner voice inspiring the cries of those who protest against unlimited war, human trafficking, environmental degradation, economic injustice, demagoguery, racism, and white nationalism. Crying in the wilderness of human waywardness, God is the persistent voice, often drowned out by greed and the lust for power, in those who perpetrate the structures of evil as well as the cautionary whisper challenging the self-righteousness, polarization, and virtue shaming of those whose vision of justice and peace leads to alienation from those whose positions and policies they challenge.

God is the Eros of the Universe, the Inner Passion of All Things, and also the Adventure of the Universe as One: no one is beyond the boundaries of God's love and quest for wholeness. God inspires passionate protest and prayerful reconciliation. God loves those whom we see, or see us, as the enemy, and enjoins us to self-transcending love that embraces, critiques, challenges, and reconciles. In God's realm and in the interdependence of life, there is no "other." God's center is everywhere as the source of personal, social, religious, scientific, and planetary evolution. No one is excluded from divine inspiration. Everyone reflects, albeit at times dimly, God's presence and deserves reverence as revealing deep down, "something of God." The Eros of the Universe inspires a politics of creative transformation and inclusion. God's quest for justice is unfinished and so should be ours. God's circle of love has no circumference and our love, lived out in acts of justice seeking and affirmation, should exclude no one, even the oppressor.

The Divine Empath. God is the Ultimate Empath feeling the totality of experience. Jesus "knows our every sorrow," as the hymn says, so we can "take it to the Lord in prayer." The Ultimate Empath is the "fellow sufferer who understands" and the joyful companion who celebrates. Whitehead charts a relational, God-centered ethic and politics. Our lives are our gifts to God. What happens in this world happens to God. God not only has the "whole world in God's hands," God also has "every feeling in God's heart." The Ultimate Empath is the Heart of the Universe beating in all things and inviting us to become large-hearted ourselves. In the evolution of the religious experience, Whitehead notes:

> The new, and almost profane, concept of the goodness of God replaces the older emphasis on the will of God. He communal religion you study the will of God in order that he may preserve you. In a purified religion…you study his goodness in order to be like him. It is the difference between the enemy you conciliate and the companion whom you imitate.[7]

As noted earlier, Whitehead, like Plato and Xenophanes before him, asserted that we become like the Gods we worship. Visions of angry, vindictive, and small spirited binary gods, inspire authoritarian religions and politics and politicians who see their vocation as being their followers' "retribution" toward God and their enemies. Descriptions of God's character as personal, large-spirited, and persuasive, rather than coercive, inspire world consciousness, adventure, and acceptance of diversity of opinion, identity, and race. The circumference of the empathetic God is nowhere; all creation finds a home in the Heart of the Universe, all people can be healed and reconciled with God and God's creation.

---

7   Whitehead, *Religion in the Making,* 40.

God's creative, erotic, responsive, and empathetic love inspires a largeness of spirit that includes friend and foe alike. To be
in alignment with God's vision is to become large spirited selves,
committed to personal growth and the expansion of human rights.
The empathetic and inclusive God inspires us to challenge unjust
laws and persons who perpetuate injustice and evil in personal
relationships and politics without polarization. We must also have
persistence and passion for the embodiment of God's moral and
spiritual arcs and not let our empathy blunt our protest. Indeed,
the more we protest and the more spirited our protests become,
the greater our attentiveness to the Divine in those against whom
we protest should be cultivated. We can see the many sides of an
issue, for example, the relationship between Israel and Palestine,
and still advocate for a peaceful solution in which Israel is safe and
secure and Palestinians have freedom and self-government. Even
the oppressor has feelings and indeed our quest for justice may
liberate the oppressor's cramped and distorted spiritual life.

One of my professors Bernard Loomer spoke of size and stature as a primary spiritual and ethical virtue. Persons of stature
incarnate and imitate God's all-embracing experience and compassion without losing passion necessary for protest.

> By size I mean the stature of a person's soul, the range
> and depth of his love, his capacity for relationships. I mean
> the volume of life you can take into your being and still main-
> tain your integrity and individuality, the intensity and variety
> of outlook you can entertain in the unity of your being with-
> out feeling defensive or insecure. I mean the strength of your
> spirit to encourage others to become freer in the development
> of their diversity and uniqueness.[8]

A politics of stature embraces political contrasts and seeks
common ground among diverse positions, looking for solutions to
society's greatest ills from the perspective of any person of integrity

8   Bernard Loomer, "S-I-Z-E is the Measure," in Harry James Cargas and
     Bernard Lee, (Religious Experience and Process Theology. Mahwah, NJ:
     Paulist Press. 1976), 70.

and goodwill. Large spirited, a politics of stature recognizes that there may be many "right" answers to our most pressing political questions and that opposing sides, even in war, may be seeking, in misguided ways, similar goals. Recognizing our finitude and bias, we look for the truth in our opponent's falsehood and the falsehood in our own truth, as theologian Reinhold Niebuhr counsels.

The Power of Love. Whitehead applauds Plato's insight, described in his cosmological dialogue the *Timaeus,* as the affirmation that the creation of the universe is the result of the victory of persuasion over force. Plato's vision of divine persuasive artistry working within the world to bring out beauty and order finds its ultimate incarnation in the life of Jesus. God's power is the power of the ideal. Every knee bows, as the apostle Paul asserts in Philippians 2:5-11, out of love not out of fear. Then and now, relational power, the power of the persuasive ideal, changes the world by appealing to the better angels of our nature. In contrast, the power of Ceaser is based on coercion. "I am your retribution," says the politician drunk on the love of power and seeking to incite his followers to abandon the way of Jesus for the vision of divine wrath. The authoritarian God and their minions seek victory rather than reconciliation and punishment rather than healing. In contrast to the threatening, retributive, and coercive authoritarian God, the relational God proclaims "I am your companion. We may differ but when we listen to the better angels of our nature, we can find common ground to heal the soul of the nation." Love is stronger than death; weakness creates enemies and demands the destruction of otherness.

God is love and embracing God's love casts out fear, as scripture proclaims. God does not and cannot fully control the creaturely world. Freedom and creativity are essential to the world with which God works. God does not rule by overwhelming power, and the elimination of creaturely self-affirmation. God wants to guide the process with passionate love and restless possibility and that should be our goal in personal life and politics as well.

God and the World. God is the primary exemplar of experience and relationship, morally, spiritually, and in the nature of things. The world in which we live, the world beloved by God and the object of God's compassionate care, is characterized by relationships, experience, and value. Experience is at the heart of reality. The universe is alive and although there are various grades of experience from quantum particles to human and angelic beings, all things are centers of experience, emerging from and responding to their environment. Like God, each moment of experience is responsive and creative, and guided by its own vision of God's aim for it. To experience is to be related and to possess inherent value. The Psalms conclude "let everything that breathes praise God." (Psalm 150:6) The heavens declare the glory of God and so do breaching Right Whales and plodding pangolins. As centers of experience, beloved by God and revealing God's deep-down presence, all things are inherently valuable. Reverence for life in all forms is the ultimate ethical goal, seldom lived up to in creaturely experience.

In the interplay of cooperation and competition, Whitehead asserts that although life is robbery, we best have good reason for destroying another life. "We have no right to deface the value experience which is the essence of the universe."[9] The non-human as well as human world has value apart from our individual or corporate interests. Environmental care for the non-human world is a necessity for followers of Whitehead; so too is environmental justice, or ecojustice, that responds to those, usually the most economically vulnerable and politically marginalized, who are the primary victims of climate change and ecological destruction. We can feed the hungry, provide healthy drinking water, comfortable housing and also ensure the survival of endangered species, clear and fresh streams and lakes, healthy coral reefs, and blue skies.

Whitehead recognizes that God's vision in an interdependent, experiential, creative, and value laden universe must adapt to the concrete realities of life. The Great Idealist is also the Ultimate

---

9   Whitehead, *Modes of Thought*, 140.

Relativist. God's vision for each moment and the communities of which we are a part is the best for that impasse, but the best, compared to the ideal, can appear to be bad.[10] Despite our love for our kin and our sense of global unity, there are moments when coercion is necessary in preventing greater violence or restraining malevolence. The protestor inconveniences persons trying to shop and attend classes. They may even create institutional chaos. Our hope is that the passion of protest is joined with respect for those with whom they disagree as well as those who sympathize with their cause, and that those who protest injustice also see the virtues of those who are the objects of protest.

God invites us to always have our eyes on the prize and also to accept the achievement of penultimate goals in the real world of politics and relationships. We must never abandon the ideal but the ideal must never undermine the good we can achieve and the evil we can prevent. As my colleague at Georgetown University, Rabbi Harold White often noted, "God created the world good, but not perfect. The good has room for growth, the perfect is complete and cannot grow or change." In the pluralism of politics, we must celebrate incremental change, affirm the best intentions of those whose compromises move the moral arc forward, and applaud politicians who do the dirty work of balancing order and novelty and change and security that makes protest possible in a free and democratic society.

Whitehead's vision of a spirituality of relationship and possibility, grounded in our alignment with God's aim at beauty, challenges us to be agents of healing and wholeness. God needs us to be God's hands and feet, God's heart and head, God's voice and touch, and our personal and political agency aims toward the realization of justice, environmental well-being, human rights, peaceful and respectful decision-making, and the quest for reconciliation. As I noted earlier, as a result of the congruence of God's love and creaturely experience, value extends beyond humankind and so we must recognize the value of the non-human world apart

---

10 Whitehead, *Process and Reality,* 244.

from human interests. Our mandate is to respond to global climate change to ensure a better world for future generations and to combat the climate crisis today. We must also work to create an ecological civilization to promote the value of non-human life. We must, in the spirit of Saint Elizabeth Ann Seton and Mahatma Gandhi, live simply so that others – including our non-human companions – may simply live. We may need to make significant sacrifices as persons and as a nation so that the planet may simply survive. This is the greatest test of non-violent, non-binary creative transformation: finding the right level of coercion when the fate of the earth is at stake and national leaders are asleep at the switch. I do not know the answer here, but it must involve both love and toughmindedness.

God's eye is truly on the sparrow. God delights in the 400 or so endangered Right Whales, many swimming off New England coasts. God feels the pain of the pangolin, endangered as a result of the desire for its meat and to produce potions for human vitality. Streams, rivers, meadows, and oceans are "thin places," spirit-filled and transparent to the divine as indigenous people and Celtic spiritual guides realized. Coral reefs are dear to God's heart and should matter to us as well.

As I write this afternoon, I discovered an ant crawling up my leg. While it would be simple to thoughtlessly crush the life out of it, the scurrying ant is truly a wondrous creation of God. Consider the millions of processes at work in the ant climbing up my leg, exploring my computer, and looking for information to share with their community. Indeed, the ant may be a scout for their colony, providing "intelligence" necessary for the colony's survival and flourishing. If God is in all things, then there is something of God in the ant; and if all things are received into God, then its industry and desire to live is part of God's experience. As the Psalmist says, everything that breathes – including ants, trees, flowers, dogs, and humans – has the capacity to praise God. (Psalm 150:6)

As I noted earlier, even for the best of causes, we cannot entirely prevent suffering and must recognize that our protests may cause suffering to those whom we challenge. Boycotts and divestment may harm the economically vulnerable more than the wealthy and powerful. We cannot succumb to "weak resignation to the evils we deplore," but in the process of social transformation we must try to cause as little suffering as possible and make allowances for those whom we will harm indirectly by our reforms. It may be impossible to fully follow Hippocrates in either medicine or politics, "first do no harm." But our quest and protest for the more perfect union must be realized with as little personal trauma as possible.

Doing "something beautiful for God," often involves short term loss for long-term healing of the nation and the planet. Even the demagogue, terrorist, white nationalist, and war maker is beloved by God and reflects, albeit dimly to us, divine artistry and God's vision of wholeness. I must repeat that as benighted and intentionally destructive as the perpetrators of war and injustice often are, there is still something of God in them, and God feels their passions and pain. On the Cross, Jesus says "God, forgive them." Forgiveness may involve challenge and protest, but healing and reconciliation are the ultimate goal in the relationships of both friend and foe.

At the end of the day, Whitehead believes that healthy religion encourages world loyalty. Spirituality enlarges our sense of self to embrace the wondrous diversity of the world. Spiritual maturity takes us beyond self-interest and nationalism to love for the planet and its creatures. We become persons of stature for whom no creature is a stranger or alien and no species abandoned by God's love. Accordingly, we cultivate our compassion in the contrasts and challenges of life. With stature and compassion as goals, we can begin the process of becoming little Christs, Bodhisattvas, and good ancestors in this lifetime and leave a positive influence on those whom we will never meet and future generations of humans and non-humans.

Thurman's Mystical Activism

Howard Thurman was a mystic of universality and unity. Following his mentor, Quaker mystic Rufus Jones, Thurman claimed the vocation of being a prophet of "affirmative mysticism," whose spirituality joins contemplation and action and protests against injustice in quest of the common good. Although universal in perspective, Thurman's mysticism was rooted in his experience as Black person growing up in America. He endured the violence and humiliation of Jim Crow. In his autobiography *With Head and Heart,* Thurman recalls experiences of a young child who believed, based on her parents' prejudice, that Black people could not feel, and sunset laws that prohibited Black persons from entering white neighborhoods after dark. Thurman tells of visiting Daytona Beach, Florida, as a parent with his two daughters, in which he had to give them a version of the "talk" that all marginalized children eventually receive from their parents, trying to explain to them why they were not allowed to enter a playground reserved for White children. He knew first hand that separate but equal was not equal but humiliating, dehumanizing, and violent. Lynchings and beatings were commonplace for African Americans who stepped out of line, even innocently, offending the written and unwritten rules of Jim Crow culture. He saw in his own life the soul-constricting impact of racism in the lives Black people in America and realized that cultivating his inner life enabled to have strength to face the indignities of White racism, much of it justified by authoritarian, racist, and violent images of God, often affirmed by Thurman's fellow Christians. In Thurman's own words:

> I have sought a way of life that could come under the influence of, and be informed by, the fruits of the inner life. The cruel vicissitudes of the social situation in which I have been forced to live in American society have made it vital for me to seek resources, or a resource to which I could have access as I sought means for sustaining the personal enterprise of my life

beyond all the ravages inflicted upon it by the brutalities of the social order.[11]

Thurman's spirituality embodied the spirit of Maya Angelou's poem, which affirms that despite the attempts of others to humiliate, marginalize, dehumanize, and keep him and the Black community down, "Still I rise!" Thurman's mysticism rose to the heavens, like the angels climbing Jacob's ladder, and then returned to earth with wisdom to change the world. He knew that his rising required the rising of the dispossessed and downtrodden, and that true freedom involved all of us rising from self-interest and racism to generosity and kinship. He also recognized the fear-based hate of those who succumbed to racism and hate, whether in the Jim Crow South or Donald Trump 2020s. For Thurman, like the First Testament prophets, mysticism leads to mission. Following the example of the prophetic tradition, authentic mysticism inspires the mystic to be God's companion in healing the world through protest and political action. The mystic feels the divine pathos (Abraham Joshua Heschel) and presents an alternative vision to the current injustices perpetrated by the wealthy and powerful (Walter Brueggemann).

The story of Isaiah provides a template for Thurman's affirmative mystic which does justice and loves mercy in response to a life-changing encounter with the Holy.

> In the year that King Uzziah died, I saw the Lord sitting on a throne, high and lofty, and the hem of his robe filled the temple. Seraphs were in attendance above him; each had six wings: with two they covered their faces, and with two they covered their feet, and with two they flew. And one called to another and said,
>
> "Holy, holy, holy is the Lord of hosts;
> the whole earth is full of his glory."

---

11 Quoted in Luther Smith, *Howard Thurman: The Mystic as Prophet* (Richmond, IN: Friends United Press, 2007), 35.

The pivots on the thresholds shook at the voices of those who called, and the house filled with smoke. And I said, "Woe is me! I am lost, for I am a man of unclean lips, and I live among a people of unclean lips, yet my eyes have seen the King, the Lord of hosts!"

Then one of the seraphs flew to me, holding a live coal that had been taken from the altar with a pair of tongs. The seraph touched my mouth with it and said, "Now that this has touched your lips, your guilt has departed and your sin is blotted out." Then I heard the voice of the Lord saying, "Whom shall I send, and who will go for us?" And I said, "Here am I; send me!"

Isaiah's mysticism is grounded in God-intoxication. He sees the whole earth as filled with God's glory. It is also confessional: Isaiah recognizes his finitude and fallibility in relationship to the universal and righteous God. Although God chooses him for a mighty task, Isaiah sees himself as part of a wounded and sinful nation, complicit in his nation's wrong doing. Isaiah is one with families evicted from their homes and starving children; he is also connected to those who commit injustice and atrocity and put self-interest ahead of concern for their neighbors' well-being. Isaiah exemplifies Thurman's quest for the realization of Common Ground in which sinfulness and fallibility is joined with recognition of God's image in all people and our responsibility to be agents of social transformation. When God calls out, "whom shall I send, who will go for us?" the chastened and healed Isaiah responds, "Here I am, send me." The Word and Wisdom of God inspires involvement not escapism, empathy not apathy, and agency not passivity in facing "the evils we deplore." God cannot liberate the oppressed or convict the powerful alone. God needs us to be the instruments of God's voice, protest, and healing in the world. God wants us to be companions and co-creators, using our God-inspired power to challenge everything that keeps others from claiming their co-creativity with God and liberating all people from the soul-stifling realities of fear, hate, injustice and alienation, whether as oppressed or oppressor. "Here we are, send us," whether to the polls, the picket line, the soup kitchen, the Halls of Congress, tutoring, or lobbying for ecojustice.

In the next several paragraphs, I will describe the roots of Thurman's contemplative activism and their importance for today's prophets and protesters. While we have made many strides toward freedom, the far horizons of ecojustice and human rights still call us forward to God's Beloved Community.

Mystical Universalism. As we reflect on Thurman's mystical activism, it is important once more to localize his mysticism in his experience of being black in America. Thurman asserts that "it has been vital for me to find within myself the door that no man could shut, to locate resources that are uniquely mine, to which I must be true if the personal enterprise of my life is to be sustained despite the ravages inflicted upon it by society."[12] The inward journey gives us resources for self-affirmation, wisdom, personal stature, integrity, and a holy pragmatism that looks toward the far horizon and yet moves forward one step at a time. Thurman's commitment to cultivating an intimate relationship with God, emerging from his childhood mysticism, enabled him "to be strong enough to carry the heavy stones of the spirit which are necessary for the foundations of the kingdom of friendly men underneath a friendly sky."[13] Thurman defines mysticism in terms of a personal encounter with a personal God that widens the mystic's scope of ethical consideration.

> For our purposes, then, mysticism is defined as the response of the individual to a personal encounter with God within his own soul. This is my working definition. Such a response is total, effecting the inner quality of the life and its outward expression as its manifestation.[14]

---

12 Ibid., Kindle Location, 113-114.
13 Ibid., Kindle Location, 116-117.
14 Ibid., Kindle Location, 177-179.

The God within is also the God all around us. Having experienced God's presence in the depths of their own soul, the mystic glimpses the signs of God's presence in all humankind, including in the lives of those who perpetrate injustice or manipulate the political system for personal or economic gain. The Infinite is the intimate. The "lung" of the universe that Thurman experienced as a child, breathes through all things, enlivening all creation, friend and foe, kin and stranger. The great Celtic saint Pelagius affirmed that in every newborn you can see the face of God. Our waywardness and personal and institutional sin cannot deface our essential relatedness to God. With the Quakers, Thurman believed that there is "something of God" in every person, and our awareness of that inner divinity reality prevents us from polarizing and dehumanizing even for the cause of justice and liberation. *Ubuntu,* "I am because of you. We are because of one another." We are all part of the wondrous and diverse artistry of Whitehead's divine "poet of the universe." When we say, "God in all things. All things in God," we are challenging the binary, in-out, friend-foe, saved-unsaved vision of the universe and human life. The heartbeat of God beats in our own hearts and also the hearts of those who see themselves as our enemies. God's energy of love gives life to plankton and pangolin, Right Whale and polar bear, cell and soul. God loves creation in its entirety, and there's nothing we can do about it. The personal God also loves those we are tempted to call enemies, and there's nothing they can do about it.

The unity of life both joins and empowers. "Blest be the tie that binds," is not just a Christian hymn, but a statement of reality. Influenced by Thurman's notion of Common Ground, the foundation of reality and the hope toward which we aspire, Martin Luther King proclaimed the divinely ordered unity of life described as Beloved Community.

> It all boils down to this, that all life is interrelated. We are caught in an inescapable network of mutuality, tied into a single garment of destiny. Whatever affects one directly affects

all indirectly. We are made to live together because of the interrelated structure of reality.[15]

For some strange reason I cannot be what I ought to be until you are what you ought to be. And you can never be what you ought to be until I am what I ought to be. That's the way God's universe is made."[16]

In the spirit of a song I learned in my college days, still powerful in my Medicare years, we can affirm that while diversity is God-given, division is a fall from grace, grounded in individualistic, binary, and coercive images of God and the world.

> We are one in the Spirit
> We are one in the Lord
> We are one in the Spirit
> We are one in the Lord
>
> And we pray that all unity
> May one day be restored
> And they'll know we are Christians
> By our love, by our love
> Yes, they'll know we are Christians
> By our love.[17]

In our quest to heal the earth, no one can be left behind, no one abandoned, and no one written off as beyond the ability to change. We can turn away from God's interdependent world and plunge into the individualistic isolationism of self-made persons or nations, but when we do, we go against the nature of the universe and God's vision of humankind and our planet. The consequences of turning away from God's interdependent world, and focusing solely on nation, race, gender, or individual gain are ob-

15 Martin Luther King, Jr. *Testament of Hope: The Essential Writings and Speeches of Martin Luther King, Jr.* (edited by James M. Washington), (New York: HarperSanFrancisco, 1986), 254.

16 Martin Luther King, Jr., *A Knock at Midnight* (New York: Warner Books), 208.

17 Peter Scholtes, "They'll Know We are Christians by our Love." (1966)

vious: climate change, incivility, individual and nationally sanctioned violence, poverty, cold and hot war, and broken lives not to mention anxiety, restlessness, and discontent among the powerful and privileged. We need, as Martin Luther King said, "strength to love" and we need the stature to see our well-being connected with the well-being of others. When we protest injustice and affirm that Black and Palestinian and GLBTQ+ and Women's lives matter along with our own lives, our protests must also embrace the healing of those who perpetrate injustice, otherwise the world we imagine will come to reflect the binary, divisive, and violent world against which we protest. As is too often the case, the oppressed becomes the oppressor, when justice seeking is contaminated by binary thinking and dehumanization of the oppressors and perpetrators of injustice. They too reflect the image of God, albeit hidden from our vision.

God's Need for Human Agency. God needs us to be God's hands and feet. God needs us, as John Lewis says, to be God's companions in the quest for justice, despite the intransigence of an unjust social order that may provoke us to violence, alienation, or apathy.

> Do not get lost in a sea of despair. Be hopeful, be optimistic. Our struggle is not the struggle of a day, a week, a month, or a year, it is the struggle of a lifetime. Never, ever be afraid to make some noise and get in good trouble, necessary trouble.

Moments of solitude that give birth to mysticism inspire seasons of noisiness and "good trouble". We think of civil rights activists crossing Edmund Pettus Bridge singing songs of faith; neurodiverse Greta Thunberg protesting in from the Swedish Parliament and alerting the world to the climate change crisis; we think of the Berrigan Brothers protesting the Vietnam War; and Cesar Chavez and Dolores Huerta marching for farmworkers. The mystic prays and then rises from prayer to protest, knowing that God needs both our prayers and picketing to change the world.

Thurman's vision of God is open and relational, and personal and global. In spite of the perorations of slave owning and white nationalist preachers, God does not ordain slavery, genocide, racism, sexism, or homophobia. Open and relational theologian Thomas Oord avers, "God can't" fully control our lives or the unfolding of history. What we do makes a difference. God calls and we, like Isaiah, have the choice to respond for or against God's vision of Shalom. Our response shapes the contours of God's further calls in our lives and the world. The call of God, always aiming at the best for that impasse, as Whitehead says, may nevertheless involve "agitating the comfortable" in order "to comfort the agitated." The Peaceable Realm requires us to pray; it may also require us to picket, protest, boycott, and divest.

We are God's hands, feet, and heart. The personal and relational God inspires us to respond personally and relationally to the injustices of our time. In contrast to authoritarian and unilateral religious and secular approaches to social change, Thurman privileges a democracy of revelation, grounded in God's presence in every life. We may fight hard, but our goal is to find common ground and seek to follow the better angels of our nature and inspire these same good angels to come forth in those whose policies work against justice and equality.

God calls us to support the co-creativity and agency of all people, acting for the greater good which joins both oppressed and oppressor in God's Common Ground. Poverty leads to powerlessness, stifled imagination, broken dreams, and low self-esteem. The call to justice embraces the spirit as well as body and aims at a world where dreams live and all people rise and take their role as God's partners in bringing forth a world of beauty.

Compassionate and Contemplative Activism. The mystic experiences the profound unity of all life, grounded in God's personal relationship with each creature. Contemplation leads to action, and as painful and conflictual as activism may appear, especially to those whose policies are the subjects of our protests, social change is grounded in the compassionate recognition that the quest for justice liberates oppressor and oppressed alike. I cannot mention this too often in a world in which even justice seekers promote incivility and alienation, privileging ideology over creative transformation and peacemaking. You can, as Jesus says, gain the world and lose your soul. The celestial surgeon operates only to heal, and not humiliate or defeat. The powerful and privileged will have to share the levers of power and alter their lifestyles for "justice to flow like waters." We will have to live more simply, eat more consciously, contribute more personally and through taxes, including a global tax, and this will mean sacrifice. But the way of Jesus sees sacrifice as the portal to abundant life and full humanity for all. Letting go is an awakening to the larger world of companionship with God and God's beloved children. We find true peace in seeing the welfare of others as essential to our own well-being.

God's goal for humankind is abundant life, or a friendly world of friendly people. Injustice blocks the energy of love from enlivening and empowering those at the margins of society, whose backs are against the wall. Accordingly, the mystic's social agenda "has to do with the removal of all that prevents God from coming to himself in the life of the individual. Whatever there is that blocks this, calls for action."[18]

Social action is a form of prayer and an act of love for perpetrator and victim of injustice alike. "For the mystic, social action is sacramental, because it is not an end in itself. Always, it is the individual who must be addressed, located and released, underneath his misery and his hunger and his destitution. That whatever may be blocking his way to his own center where his altar may be found, this must be removed."[19] In this spirit, pastor and senator Raphael Warnock asserted your vote is a "prayer for the world we desire" and that democracy is the "political enactment of a spiritual idea," that everyone possesses a divine spark.

The mystic recognizes that rich and poor, and oppressor and oppressed, may be equally alienated from their deepest selves, de-

---

18 Ibid., Kindle location, 244-245.
19 Ibid., Kindle location, 249-251.

spite their economic and social differences. The soul-destroying nature of poverty and injustice is obvious and must be addressed immediately with wise personal and political action, which eventually liberates the privileged to experience the common ground of Beloved Community.

To repeat, social change is always painful for those who have perpetuated injustice. The perpetrators of injustice or those who benefit from the privileges of race, gender, economics, or nation of origin are often oblivious to their complicity in social evil and personal pain. Often, they (or we, and here I am confessing my own complicity and apathy) rationalize injustice by saying that "there's nothing we can do about it," "what can one person do," or that "it's just the way things are." The emergence of empathy can be painful because empathy alerts us both to the pain of others and the negative impact of our actions on those who suffer as a result of their (and our) unconscious, though often intended, racism, sexism, and materialism. In Thurman's language, those who perpetrate injustice intentionally or as result of apathy and greed may need to be "shocked" out of their complacency, sense of entitlement, and assumptions of privilege and superiority through confrontation acts of protest, picketing, and boycotts is to awaken them to their intimate connection with those whom they knowingly or unknowingly harm. The goal of political challenge is not to defeat the powerful but awaken them to the healing power of God's vision of Shalom, Beloved Community, and Common Ground that joins all of us. In Thurman's words:

> What is important for the mystic is that the purpose of the shock treatment is to hold before the offender a mirror that registers an image of himself, that reflects the image of those who suffer at his hands. The total function of such action is to tear men from any alignments that prevent them from putting themselves in the other person's place, but it must never be forgotten that the central concern of the mystic is to seek to remove anything that prevents the individual

from free and easy access to his own altar-stair that is in his own heart.[20]

Beyond the binary is the relational. Beyond injustice is community. The relational and loving God inspires us to be "godlike" in our embrace of the powerful and privileged "other" whether that "other" be an Israeli political leader bent on blood lust, a Hamas terrorist, a prevaricating and divisive USA politician, white nationalist, self-made capitalist, or progressive ideologue. The healing of the oppressor – and at times, protesters can tragically embrace the path of coercion, domination, and division - becomes a catalyst for the embodiment of God's vision of Shalom in daily interactions and political and business decision-making.

Choosing to become agents of social transformation can put prophets and activists at risk. Contemplative activists, such as Oscar Romero, Dorothy Day, and Martin Luther King, are often the objects of hatred and persecution in their lifetimes and must wait till their deaths to be seen as harbingers of a new and better humanity. Even if the mystic must suffer for the cause of justice, "a way has to be found to restore and discover self-worth, authentic identity, the chief manifestation… of the in-dwelling presence of which the mystic speaks."[21] In this way, the mystic achieves her or his spiritual goal, that all may experience holiness and, in so doing, God will be "all in all" (1 Corinthians 15:28).

Common Ground

In the quest to heal the soul of the nation and the planet, two statements from Whitehead, previously quoted in this text, are particularly insightful.

> [God's] purpose is always embodied in the particular ideals relevant to the actual state of the world. Thus all attainment is immortal in that it fashions the actual ideas which

---

20 Ibid., Kindle location, 270-274.
21 Ibid., Kindle location, 335-337.

are God in the world as it is now. Every act leaves the world
with a deeper or fainter impress of God. He then passes into
his next relation to the world with enlarged, or diminished,
presentation of ideal values.[22]

The initial aim [God's vision for each moment of experience in its particular context] is the best for that impasse. But
if the best be bad, the ruthlessness of God can be personified
as Até, the goddess of mischief.[23]

These challenging passages set the stage for understanding the
quest for common ground in political and communal life. First,
they assert that God is *not* fully in control of the details of our communities and our personal lives. While God provides framework
for the evolving and interdependent universe and is the inspiration of the moral and spiritual arcs of history, human beings – and
all occasions of experience – have the freedom to turn toward or
away from God's vision of truth, beauty, and goodness. To repeat,
"every act leaves the world with a deeper or fainter impress of God.
He then passes into his next relation to the world with enlarged,
or diminished, presentation of ideal values."[24] We have the power
to block the ever-flowing stream of justice. We can divert God's
universal vision to suit our own private and national self-interest,
thus negatively shaping the contours of God's vision and power
in the world. To repeat, God is not the source of slavery, human
trafficking, and war. These result from self-interest, individualism,
and the quest for power and prosperity at the expense of others.
We cannot limit God's vision, but we can limit God's incarnation
in our world. We can crucify God's vision to attain the false and
unsatisfying devices and desires of our own hearts and national
pride. Still, in spite of setbacks in the quest for Beloved Community, God never gives up on us or the world. God is the "fellow
sufferer who understands" and also the "prophetic presence" who

---

22 Whitehead, *Religion in the Making.*, 152.
23 Whitehead, *Process and Reality,* 244.
24 Whitehead, *Religion in the Making.*, 152.

calls us to new forms of community, economics, and politics to expand the vision of abundant life to embrace all creation.

God's aim is "the best for that impasse" but the best may seem "bad" to those holding to power or those whose ideologies divide the world into friend and foe and winner and loser. In those cases, the movements of God in the world may seem like divine "mischief," when in fact what appears to be "ruthless" to the powerful and domineering is God's own presence in our lives and the world inspiring "good trouble, necessary trouble" that confronts our ideologies, privilege, power, and violence with the "shock" of a spiritual and political higher aspiration and the pragmatic vision of a new earth. Birthing a new earth is painful – "creation groans" in hope for healing, as the apostle Paul says – and yet we are to be bold and humble midwives of new creation in ourselves, our movements, our communities, our nation, and the world. This "growing edge" shapes both the process and goal of political action and social change. In the next few paragraphs, we will consider the embodiment of Whitehead's and Thurman's vision in transforming our social order and explore where their visions take us in our time of turmoil, incivility, and potential political, economic, and environmental catastrophe.

Social activist A.J. Muste once said, "...there is no way to peace. Peace is the way." The personal and relational God affirmed by Thurman and Whitehead promotes, in "the fierce urgency of now," proclaimed by Martin Luther King, vigorous and full-spirited quests for social and political change grounded in respect for and affirmation of personality and relationships. Do not diminish or destroy the creaturely value at the basis of existence, counsels Whitehead. See the divine in those who differ from us, challenges Thurman. As I have contended throughout this text, authoritarian politics are by nature binary and dehumanizing. They eventually lead to violence and exclusion. In religion, the unilateral coercive deity authorizes us to dominate and coerce others to achieve our political goals. In contrast, the "shock" of protest, inspired by a relational vision of the universe and its Creative Wisdom, is accompanied by reverence and respect for all concerned, even in tragic times of conflict. "Blessed are the peacemakers for they will be called the children of God" (Matthew 5:9). We must seek the peace of self-transcendence and empathy in the quest for a world in which no one, rich or poor, is left behind.

Whitehead and Thurman proclaim a metaphysics of love that inspires loving social transformation. Loving Wisdom constantly creates the universe, awakening the love in us. Loving Compassion embraces the world in its joy and pain, modeling empathy in citizens and their political leaders. Religion is world loyalty, which calls us to love the world, especially in the conflicts of politics and social transformation. In times of conflict, we must seek with all our hearts to follow the better angels of our nature so that we will not succumb to the evil we see in others. Again, listen to the words of Jesus, which no doubt inspired the theological and ethical visions of Thurman and Whitehead.

> You have heard that it was said, "You shall love your neighbor and hate your enemy." But I say to you: Love your enemies and pray for those who persecute you, so that you may be children of your Father in heaven, for he makes his sun rise on the evil and on the good and sends rain on the righteous and on the unrighteous. For if you love those who love you, what reward do you have? Do not even the tax collectors do the same? And if you greet only your brothers and sisters, what more are you doing than others? Do not even the gentiles do the same? Be perfect, therefore, as your heavenly Father is perfect. (Matthew 5:43-48)

To be "perfect" is to have the spiritual stature and the consequent ability to embrace otherness and diversity in the midst of conflict. To embrace divine perfection is to be both creative and responsive in your relationality. To make a difference in the world and to listen to your deepest needs and the deepest needs of those around you. While we must always keep our eyes on the prize of justice and equality and planetary healing, we must also affirm small steps in the slow process of realizing God's Realm on earth as it is in heaven. We must remember in our idealism, that the perfect is often the enemy of the good, when we refuse to be like God who continues to present "enlarged or diminished" ideal values to those whom God loves and whom we are called to love. God struggles with injustice and does not succumb to hate, and so should we. We must stride toward freedom, treasuring every step forward even as we keep our eyes always on the prize of the Peaceable Realm. In this regard, Thurman tells of President John Hope's counsel when he felt disappointment at the penultimate values of his White companions.

> During his senior year, Thurman accompanied Hope to an interracial meeting at a local   YMCA   branch,   with some black educational leaders and a handful of white liberals…one white man announced proudly that the segregated meeting had been changed so that it would be divided vertically, with the center aisle as the demarcation line in the main area and balcony. [Disgusted Thurman walked out] Hope followed him and told him by Thurman's account, "I know how you feel about what's going on in there, but you must remember that these are the best and most liberal men in the entire South. We must work with them. There is no one else. Remember.[25]

Apostles of the butterfly effect, Whitehead and Thurman believed that small acts, even imperfect and penultimate acts, can transform the world. As Jewish mystics say, "if you save one soul, it's as if you've saved the world." I would amend this to say, "if you save one moment with compassion or care, it's as if you've saved the world." Treasuring small achievements opens the door to new possibilities. To paraphrase one of my favorite statements from Dag Hammarskjold, Secretary General of the United Nations from 1953-1961, "For all that has been – the achievements, small and large, that have changed society – thanks! For all that shall be in realizing God's dream of Shalom by new achievements

---

25 Paul Harvey, *Howard Thurman and the Disinherited: A Religious Biography* (Grand Rapids: William B. Eerdman's Publishing, 2020), 25.

in the quest for justice and healing – yes!"[26] In committing ourselves to God's all-inclusive vision of Shalom and treasuring each step toward Beloved Community, we become the great "yes" of the future and, as June Jordan says of women marching against South African apartheid, "the ones we have been waiting for," bringing about the world we have been waiting for.

Thurman was well aware of the need for self-awareness among the prophets of social change. "As a Christian, I must see to it that what I condemn in society, I do not permit to grow and flow in me."[27] Awareness of our own inner temptation to incivility and violence, our own prejudice and binary thinking, is essential if we are to create a social order where everyone belongs and is seen as God's beloved child. Still, we must go forth, like Isaiah, in all our imperfection, aligning ourselves God's aim at beauty and the moral and spiritual arcs of the universe. Whitehead's and Thurman's vision of a value-laden, experiential, interdependent universe, inspired by a personal and relational God, promotes the affirmation of democracy, environmental well-being and the ethical consideration of non-humans, affirmation and promotion of human diversity in race, ethnicity, and sexuality, hospitality toward immigrants and asylum seekers, economic well-being and educational excellence for all regardless of race or class, and political processes that ensure that rights and responsibilities are coordinated for the well-being of the community. We must become the prophets of a truly Ecological Civilization, shaping the planet as a whole and seeking wholeness for humankind and the non-human world in all their variety.

At the end of the day, our goal is Common Ground, or Beloved Community, achieved through the process of prophetic healing that embraces everyone and affirms God's presence in every member of the social order. God's continual quest for wholeness gives rise to hope for the future, despite the overwhelming challenges we face to heal the planet and our nation. God will not

26 Dag Hammarsjold, *Markings* (New York: Knopf, 1964, 89
27 Ibid., 98,

give up, nor should we, though the horizons of God's Realm seem far off. Still, we dream of the day and our contemplations give birth to actions, when, as the prophet Isaiah says:

> The wolf shall live with the lamb;
>   the leopard shall lie down with the kid;
> the calf and the lion will feed together,
>   and a little child shall lead them.
> The cow and the bear shall graze;
>   their young shall lie down together;
>   and the lion shall eat straw like the ox.
> The nursing child shall play over the hole of the asp,
>   and the weaned child shall put its hand on the adder's den.
> They will not hurt or destroy
>   on all my holy mountain,
> for the earth will be full of the knowledge of the Lord
>   as the waters cover the sea...
> They shall beat their swords into plowshares
>   and their spears into pruning hooks;
> nation shall not lift up sword against nation;
>   neither shall they learn war any more.
> (Isaiah 11:6-9:2:4)

Awakening to God's Growing Edge

Thurman and Whitehead see social transformation as grounded in our encounter with the Holy in our lives and in the universe. Both believed a recovery of Jesus' vision is essential to the transformation of Christianity from a religion of the status quo to a faith of adventurous global transformation. In this first exercise, we will reflect on Jesus' mission statement, recorded in Luke 4:18-19. In Jesus' first public address he invokes the countercultural vision of the prophet Isaiah, contrasting with the violence of the Roman Empire and the exclusivism of many of his Jewish kin.

God's Spirit is Upon You. Take time to read Jesus' words twice contemplatively. Then, if health and time permit, take the scripture out for a walk or imaginatively see the moving power of the scripture. When we move our bodies or visualize new horizons, new possibilities emerge, unhindered by confining traditions.

> The Spirit of the Lord is upon me,
> because he has anointed me
> to bring good news to the poor.
> He has sent me to proclaim release to the captives
> and recovery of sight to the blind,
> to set free those who are oppressed,
> to proclaim the year of the Lord's favor.
> (Luke 4:18-19)

As you walk contemplatively or visualize while sitting, awaken to God's Spirit moving in your life. Feel God's Spirit enter with every breath and move forward with every footstep. Prayerfully consider the questions, "Toward what new possibilities is God's Spirit calling you? What would it mean for you to embody Jesus' mission of good news, release, healing, and liberation? What first steps might you take to be God's companion in transforming the world, led by Jesus' vision of Shalom?" Conclude by giving thanks for God's constantly inspiring Spirit and the energy and wisdom to embody God's Spirit in the world.

Taking a Beauty Break to Bring Beauty to the World. Theologian Patricia Adams Farmer counsels busy and socially involved persons like us to take a "beauty break." As we participate in the long-promised road to justice, we need the replenishment and rejuvenation that comes from beauty. Beauty invites us to be amazed at the wonders, the micro and the macro, of the cells of our bodies and the galaxies without number. In walking with beauty all around us, as the Navajo (Dine) blessing prayer advises, we can perspective, transcend self-interest, and identify ourselves with the well-being of the planet.

Following the near fatal stabbing of Martin Luther King in Harlem, Thurman felt "an awareness that would not leave" and alerted his wife Sue, "Tomorrow morning I'm going down to New York to see Martin. I am not sure, but I must talk to him personally if the doctors permit." They talked about his physical condition and Thurman "urged [Martin] to extend the period [of convalescence] by an additional two weeks. This would give him time away from the immediate pressure of the movement to reassess himself in relation to the cause, to rest his body and mind with healing detachment, and to take a long look that only solitary brooding can provide."[28]

In the maelstrom of family and professional life and social action, we need time for solitude to immerse our souls in beauty and find refreshment and rejuvenation for the journey ahead. Take a beauty break. Bathe your senses in the world around you. Notice, wonder, be amazed, and give thanks for this good earth as you commit yourself to being God's hands and feet in healing the planet and its creatures. You can take a five-minute, afternoon, or week-long beauty break to rejuvenate your spirit for the prophetic journey ahead.

A Prayer from the Growing Edge

Social transformation is an act of hope that history holds the seeds of transformation and that a holy adventure awaits us even in times of crisis and limitation.

I will make an act of faith toward all mankind,
Where doubts would linger and suspicions brood.
I will make an act of joy toward all sad hearts,
Where laughter pales and tears abound.
I will make an act of strength toward feeble things,
Where life grows dim and death draws near.
I will make an act of trust toward all life,

28 Thurman, *With Head and Heart*, 254-255

Where fears preside and distrusts keep watch.
I will make an act of love toward friend and foe,
Where trust is weak and fear burns bright.
I make a deed to God of all my days –
And look out upon life with quiet eyes.[1]

---

1   Howard Thurman, *The Mood of Christmas, 26.*

CHAPTER SIX

LIVING A HOLY ADVENTURE

At the heart of the nature of things, there are always the dream of youth and the harvest of tragedy. The Adventure of the Universe starts with the dream and reaps Tragic Beauty. This is the secret of the union of Zest with Peace: - That the suffering attains its end in a Harmony of Harmonies. The immediate experience of this Final Fact, with its union of Youth and Tragedy, is the sense of Peace. In this way the world receives its persuasion toward such perfections as are possible for its diverse individual occasions.[2]

The true meaning of Christmas is expressed in the sharing of one's graces in a world in which it is so easy to become callous, insensitive, and hard. Once this spirit becomes part of a man's life, every day is Christmas, and every night is freighted with anticipation of a fresh, and perhaps holy, adventure.[3]

My theological and spiritual relationships with Whitehead and Thurman have been among the most significant adventures of my life. Both have been near at hand, shaping the contours of my world view and spiritual practices, and inviting me to become an innovative theologian, pastor, and spiritual guide. They have been guides in my own holy adventure

2   Whitehead, *Adventures of Ideas,* 296.
3   Howard Thurman, *The Mood of Christmas* (New York: Harper & Row, 1973), 19.

as a theologian, pastor, spiritual guide, and writer, not to mention husband, father and grandfather, and citizen.

My relationship with Thurman is personal. In the past few years, I have discovered that two of Thurman's closest friends, Allan Armstrong Hunter and George L. "Shorty" Collins, were among my wife's and my most significant spiritual mentors. I knew they were Thurman's acquaintances but I was unaware of the pivotal nature of their relationships for the three of them until I read Thurman's *With Head and Heart.*

As a result of her participation in the Fellowship of Reconciliation, the oldest peace and justice organization in the United States, Allan Armstrong Hunter mentored Kate as a seminary student at Claremont School of Theology. From Hunter, Kate learned simple meditative practices, mindfulness exercises, and the prayer in the final section of this book. "Shorty" Collins – Rev. "Shorty" as he was known at San Jose State University – was college pastor and draft counselor when I sought Conscientious Objector status during the Vietnam War. "Shorty" invited me and another student to assist him in a nursing home worship service and two weeks later put the task in our hands, planting the seeds that led to ordained ministry.

As I noted earlier, I first encountered Thurman and Whitehead in 1972, one in a public lecture, the other in a class. As a recently returned Christian, whose faith was a hodge podge of Hinduism, Buddhism, and Transcendentalism, who had found his way back to the church through unlikely portal of Transcendental Meditation, I was looking for a creative synthesis of my global spirituality with my growing involvement in Progressive Christianity. Whitehead provided a path for the mind, a holistic vision of an intimate God, active in the world yet needed our partnership to heal the earth. Thurman provided a path with a heart, to quote Carlos Castenada's Native American spiritual guide Don Juan, that would join contemplation and action. In the creative synthesis of Whitehead and Thurman, I could seamlessly join head, heart, and hands, a God I could believe in and a spirituality that joined East and West and inspired the quest for justice. I believe that the wisdom of Whitehead and Thurman inspire a global Christianity, progressive and world affirming in spirit, and responsive to the social, political, and planetary crises of our times in ways that encourage common ground among diverse groups and political perspectives.

In this concluding chapter, we will consider how we can embark on a holy adventure of social transformation with Whitehead and Thurman as our guides and companions. This adventure will involve the heart and hands, emotion and service, as well as the head, intellect and theological reflection in its focus on experiencing the wisdom of these two theological and spiritual guides. Thurman and Whitehead are, as Yoruba spirituality affirms, "good ancestors," who live on in my life and in the progressive quest to heal the world and the soul of our nation.

Whitehead and Thurman believe that we are already on a holy adventure and may not be aware of it. God is moving in our lives and the moral and spiritual arcs are flowing in and through us. A story in the Sufi tradition recounts the adventure of a man who lived in Baghdad and dreamed of a treasure buried under a house in Cairo. With excitement, he set out on a great adventure, encountering numerous ordeals on the way. Despite the challenges, he persisted and eventually found the house in Cairo that he had visualized in his dream. He engaged the homeowner in conversation, sharing the contours of the dream that inspired his pilgrimage. On hearing the man's dream, the owner of the house responded that on the previous night, he had dreamed about a house in Baghdad under which a great treasure was buried. The traveler recognized that it was his own home and, returning home, found the treasure he was seeking that had been buried there all along. The Cairo homeowner, no doubt, also discovered treasure right in his own backyard. As the slave preacher proclaimed, you are a child of God. Right here and now, God is in you and with you. You have what you need to be free and creative in bringing God's Realm to birth in your life, relationships, and political involvement. You can venture forth to other worlds, and also take the journey without distance in awakening to the infinity of your spirit. You are God's child, your life is a treasure, and there is nothing you or anyone else can do about it!

In the following paragraphs, I outline the spiritual, emotional, and theological contours of a holy adventure outlined by Whitehead and Thurman.

Passion and Eros. Thurman and Whitehead assert that passion is essential to living out our potential, individually and as agents of God's Vision of Beauty and Peace. Whitehead asserts that there is a Divine Eros inspiring our personal and planetary adventures providing lures or aims for each moment of experience. The aim of the universe is toward the production of beauty, and that aim is moving within our lives. The dream of youth inspires us to adventures of ideas and social transformation. Martin Luther King proclaims, "I have a dream" and then gets down to the hard work of bringing the dream of social justice and equality to reality. Thurman counsels seekers to follow their passions: "Don't ask what the world needs. Ask what makes you come alive, and go do it. Because what the world needs is people who have come alive." With the early Christian theologian Irenaeus, Thurman and Whitehead believe that the glory of God is a person fully alive. Fully alive people – mystics, artists, poets, musicians, theologians, children, and every day adventurers – want the world to come alive. They are not content with merely living, but as Whitehead avers, they want to live well, and then live better, and share that quest with others. The passionate life inspires us to further the passions, hopes, and dreams of others, and this requires a friendly world of friendly people, a place of common ground in which our joys and sorrows are one, and we challenge everything that stands in the way of full humanity.

The passionate life, inspired by our experience and commitment to the Divine Eros, imagines a world of possibility and then makes it happen. This may require mentoring, creativity, and teaching. It may also require prophetic good trouble to create an environment where all people can aspire to be fully human.

As Frederic Buechner asserts, a person's calling is the intersection where your deep gladness meets the deep hunger of the world. Prayer, passion, and patience give wings to our dreams and then plant them on the ground of social change. In bringing justice and equality to the world, we enable children and their parents to imagine great things for themselves and the world and then plant their dreams on solid ground. We become passionate peacemakers, joyful justice seekers, and ecstatic environmentalists.

Empathy. "Howard, you can't feel," said the young girl who stuck Thurman with a hat pin after he admonished her for interfering with his leaf raking. Feeling is at the heart of reality for both Thurman and Whitehead. Experience is universal, feeling is universal, and value is universal. In relational and political life, alignment with the universe mandates empathy even when we must make difficult decisions. In a feeling universe, everything is personal, and nothing is abstract. We shape one another by our words, actions, and social policies. We have, according to Whitehead, no right to (unthinkingly and intentionally) deface the feeling value of the universe. It goes without saying that social transformation evokes a variety of feelings and may cause pain to those who are the object of boycotts, protests, and infringement upon what they think are their "God-given" rights. While we must follow where the moral and spiritual arcs of history lead, we must do our best to minimize the harm we cause in the quest for justice. We must also recognize that we will on occasion cause pain, often to those who are already the most vulnerable. We must also recognize that even in the quest for justice, we may cause pain to the "fellow sufferer who understands." God feels the pain of the rich and powerful as well as the dispossessed. Our hope in political action is not only to affirm the universality of value but seek as much as possible non-violent and non-coercive solutions to political and economic conflict as well as foreign policy. The aim of the Adventurous and Friendly Society (my combination of Whitehead's and Thurman's social goals) is to bring joy to children and the adults who care for them, to nurture feelings of safety, to provide for basic human needs, and build the foundation for hopes and dreams. Big hearts, the heart of Jesus and the Bodhisattva, join big minds that produce large spirited public policies and theological perspectives that heal bodies, minds, and spirits.

Agency and Creativity. The maximization of freedom and creativity are at the heart of the universe and the Common Ground we seek. The Empathetic and Relational God encourages freedom. God is not a unilateral and authoritarian sovereign but a supportive companion who delights in our achievements. Like a good parent, God wants us to grow in wisdom, stature, freedom, and agency. Our agency expands God's agency. When we embody in concrete actions our passion for the possible, God is able to be more active in God's quest for beauty of experience and a social order promoting freedom and creativity. Freedom is real, agency is real, and creativity is real. Even when we cannot alter external circumstances, we can alter our attitude, claiming freedom in spite of the limitations others place on us. The healthy social order encourages as much freedom and creativity as possible congruent with the well-being of the community.

In the world of Whitehead and Thurman, rights are always mated with responsibilities, whether we are talking about capitalism, gun ownership, speech, private property, or protest. Social reformers should be encouraged to protest injustice with open spirits. As I counseled earlier, they should also be mindful of situations where protest leads to unwarranted inconvenience, destruction of property, or puts vulnerable persons at risk, and do their best to minimize unnecessary pain even as they embody the spirit of good trouble. There is no clear formula for the calculus of rights and responsibilities either in social protest, individual freedom, or property ownership but we should always take into consideration the impact of our actions on the common good, the environment, public safety, and the feelings of others. We must as much as possible sacrifice our individualistic self-interest, and our desire to defeat the opponent, for world loyalty.

Gentle Providence. Whitehead and Thurman affirm a providential universe in which God's vision is present in every moment of experience. In his autobiography, *With Head and Heart*, Thurman describes several providential moments that shaped and inspired his spiritual adventures: learning about Jesus from his Grandmother Nancy Ambrose, encountering a working man at a train station who gave him enough money to continue his journey to one of three high schools available to African Americans in Florida, spending an afternoon with Gandhi, the invitation to the co-pastor the first intentionally interracial congregation in the United States, the Church of the Fellowship of All Peoples, and the call to be Dean of the Chapel at Boston University, the first African American to be a senior administrator at a primarily White university. Nearing retirement in Great Britain, Whitehead providentially received the invitation to teach philosophy with complete freedom at Harvard University, enabling him to embody the Platonic quest for a living and adventurous cosmology. Providence guides our lives and the contours of history without coercion or predestination and to those who attune themselves with God's movements in their lives and society, "nothing walks with aimless feet." Although we may not discern in real time providential moments in our nation's or planet's history, we need to be attentive to possibilities for radical transformation: the passage of the New Deal and Civil Rights legislation, the tearing down of the Berlin Wall, global climate accords, the Supreme Court decision related to Marriage Equality. As we ponder future providential moments, we cannot always, as Theodore Parker confesses, discern the moral arc of history but God's vision marches on beside us and those glimpse the contours of non-coercive and invitational Divine Providence shout, "Glory, Glory, Hallelujah!" In the intricate interdependence of life, we may be the answer to someone's prayer or a people's prayer by our compassionate action and faithful listening and responding.

Healing the Planet. While neither Whitehead nor Thurman spoke at length about environmental issues, both recognized that we live in a universe in which the heavens declare the glory of God and so do the cells of our bodies. Thurman speaks of the world as one great lung, breathing through all of us, and like the Celtic spirit persons, Thurman experienced an oak tree as a thin place where he could share his deepest concerns. In his later writings and conversations, Thurman recognizes the need for an ecological society that balances human need and the well-being of the non-human world. Nature is alive. Experience and value are ubiquitous, apart from human interests. All things are interconnected and shape one another. Deep down, the reality that there is no "other" includes our relationships with the non-human as well as human worlds.

We cannot separate human well-being from non-human well-being. It is not accidental that the first full-length book focusing on the theology of ecology, *Is It Too Late?*, was written by a process theologian and second generation follower of Whitehead John B. Cobb, Jr. Keenly aware of the realities of injustice that plague the economically disadvantaged and are evident in terms of greater incidence of respiratory illness not to mention toxins in the water supply, Thurman's world view is foundational for ecojustice. We must heal the planet concurrently with our quest for economic and social justice, including justice for the two-thirds of the developing world. Whatever stands in the way of persons realizing their full potential as God's beloved children must be challenged by mystics and politically involved persons of faith.

Companioning God. Whitehead and Thurman both posit a God-filled universe and a God-centered basis for ethics and social justice. The universe and human life are not a tale told by an idiot signifying nothing but the theatre of divine creativity and wisdom, aiming at the production of beauty of experience, just social structures, and formation of Beloved Community. God is the source of the passion for justice and value. When the slave preacher spoke to his brutalized and dehumanized congregation, telling them that they are God's children, created in God's image, he was speaking on behalf of God. While God ensures the order of the universe, seed time and harvest, God is also the source of the prophetic passion for justice. The Ultimate Empath, God is intimately involved in the suffering and joy we experience. God guides the moral and spiritual arcs of human life, and the universe, in a relational non-coercive manner. God is the energy of novelty and justice, and not the sanction of the status quo. The Source of Possibility, God presents us with the prophetic vision of "justice rolling down like waters and righteousness like an ever-flowing stream." (Amos 5:24) God's power is found in love and not coercion. While Thurman does not, to my knowledge, address the fine points of divine power, it is clear that his focus on contemplative activism is grounded in an open and relational universe characterized by creaturely freedom and creativity. Metaphysically speaking, God calls us to wider circles of freedom and agency. God is the inspiration of justice-seeking and prophetic action. Always calling us forward, God is never the ground of the unjust status quo.

A relational God inspires the passion for justice. God encourages the agency of the mystic who seeks to eliminate everything that stands between persons and their destiny as God's beloved children. Accordingly, luring us toward new horizons of Shalom, God is the ultimate inspiration for prophetic restlessness and challenge and the transformation of our ecclesiastical and political institutions. God's power is that of the ideal, as Whitehead avers, and the ideals God presents are always at odds with the current social order. When we believe we have reached the "more perfect union," God responds with the words "*Plus Ultra* - there is more" to be done to heal the world and liberate the possibilities of the human and non-human world. God can't do this alone, but needs prophetic voices, compassionate care givers, prayerful protesters, and persistent peacemakers. When God asks, "whom shall I send?" to respond to injustice, incivility, and environmental destruction, will we respond, "Here we are, send us?"

Peace and Self-Transcendence. Whitehead asserts that religion is ultimately about world loyalty. Authentic religious experience expands our sense of self far beyond self-interest to embrace the well-being of others and ultimately the well-being of the planet and beyond. In similar fashion, Thurman recognizes that mystical experiences liberate us from the small defensive self to identify ourselves with God's Spirit flowing in the mystic and all creatures. Mysticism broadens rather than reduces our scope of ethical concern and deepens our empathy for our human and non-human world. From this perspective, contemplative political activism both reflects and deepens the quality of our relationship to the Holy and our planetary companions. Whitehead and Thurman recognize that a holy unrest may contribute to the transformation of the social order: we can picket and pray and experience peace within protest. In the spirit of Psalm 46, we can "be still and know" God's presence in the social evils we face, challenge our self-interest and myopia, and gain a self as large as the universe, the self of Jesus and the Buddhist Bodhisattva. In words that echo Jesus' wisdom, for whoever wants to save their life will lose it, but whoever loses their life for me will find it" (Matthew 16:25), Whitehead affirms that in letting go the limited self, we experience the peace that passes all understanding, even in conflict and tragedy.

> Peace is the removal of inhibition and not its introduction. It results in a wider sweep of conscious interest. It enlarges the field of attention. Thus, peace is self-control at its widest, - at the width where the 'self' has been lost and interest has been transferred to coordinations wider than the personality...Peace is the understanding of tragedy, and the same time its preservation.[5]

The contemplative activist recognizes both the tragic sense of life and the wonder of all creation. Greater empathy means the experience of greater pain and also and deeper joy, so that we can "rejoice," as the apostle Paul does in his writing from prison to the community at Philippi, knowing that our lives and all creation are embraced in God's Holy Adventure.

> At the heart of the nature of things, there are always the dream of youth and the harvest of tragedy. The Adventure of

---

5   Alfred North Whitehead, *Adventures of Ideas* (New York: Free Press, 1933), 285-286.

the Universe starts with the dream and reaps Tragic Beauty. This is the secret of the union of Zest with Peace: - That the suffering attains its end in a Harmony of Harmonies. The immediate experience of this Final Fact, with its union of Youth and Tragedy, is the sense of Peace. In this way the world receives its persuasion toward such perfections as are possible for its diverse individual occasions.[6]

We can experience, in the spirit of the African American Spiritual, sung by persons whose lives were encompassed by slavery, "I've got peace like a river...I've got joy like an ocean...I've got love like a fountain," when we dedicate head, heart, and hands to God's inclusive love and global vision. Peace is the gift of relationship with the Heart of the Universe which beats in our hearts and hearts of all creation, a melody of love and calls us to common ground with all creation. In all of life's challenges, we can affirm the final words of Thurman's autobiography, "there is a secret door which leads into the central place, where the Creator of Life and the God of the Human Heart are one and the same. I take my stand for the future and for generations who follow over the bridges we have already crossed. It is here that the meaning of the hunger of the heart is unified. The Head and Heart at last inseparable; they are lost in the wonder of the One."[7] And let the people shout, "Free at last, free at last, God all-loving, we're free at last. Amen."

Awakening to God's Growing Edge

We conclude this text once more with a focus on breathing with God. The universe is one great lung breathing in and through us. When we breathe deeply, we connect with the Risen Jesus breathing on his followers and the winds of the Spirit on Pentecost. Every breath can be a prayer in a world in which every creature has the ability to praise God. In this exercise, take a few moments to breathe deeply, then read Allan Armstrong Hunter's

6   Ibid., 296.
7   Thurman, *With Head and Heart,* 269.

prayer, letting it fill your spirit, and then breathe deeply, opening
to Hunter's poetic vision.

> I breathe your blue sky deeply in
> To blow it gladly back again.
> I breathe your shining beauty in
> To call forth the buried talent in me.
> I breathe your healing energy in
> To vibrate through each body cell.
> We breathe your reconciling spirit in
> To bring peace in us, and in the world.
> We breathe your resurrection power in
> To make our relationships new and glad.
> We breathe your strength and warmth and humor in
> To share joyously with all we meet.

A Prayer from the Growing Edge

Let us go forth knowing that the spirit of God's Growing
Edge, God's incarnation in the world continues, and that the Spirit of Christmas, of new life in the face of death, moves through our
lives and history growing in us and the world.

> When the song of the angels is stilled,
> when the star in the sky is gone,
> when the kings and princes are home,
> when the shepherds are back with their flocks,
> the work of Christmas begins:
> to find the lost,
> to heal the broken,
> to feed the hungry,
> to release the prisoner,
> to rebuild the nations,
> to bring peace among the people,
> to make music in the heart.[8]

---

8   Howard Thurman, *The Mood of Christmas,* 23

BIBLIOGRAPHY

Thurman Related Texts

Peter Eisenstadt, *Against the Hounds of Hell: A Life of Howard Thurman*. Charlottesville, VA: 2021.

Bruce Epperly, *Prophetic Healing: Howard Thurman's Vision of Contemplative Activism*, Friends United Press, 2020.

_____, *The Work of Christmas: The Twelve Days of Christmas with Howard Thurman*, Anamchara Books, 2017.

Paul Harvey, *Howard Thurman and the Disinherited: A Religious Biography* Grand Rapids: William Eerdmans Publishing Company, 2020.

C. Anthony Hunt, *Blessed are the Peacemakers: A Theological Analysis of the Thoughts of Howard Thurman and Martin Luther King, Jr.* Lima, OH: Wyndham Hall Press, 2005.

_____, *Come Go with Me: Howard Thurman and a Gospel of Radical Inclusivity* (Lima, OH: Wyndham Hall Press, 2019.

Luther E. Smith, *Howard Thurman: The Mystic as Prophet* Richmond, IN: Friends United Press, 1993.

Howard Thurman, *Apostles of Sensitiveness.* Boston: American Unitarian Association, 1956.

_____, *The Centering Moment.* Richmond, IN: Friends United Press, 1969.

_____, *The Creative Encounter.* Richmond, IN: Friends United Press, 1954.

_____, *Deep is the Hunger.* (New York: Harper and Brothers, 1951.

_____, *Deep River and the Negro Spiritual Speaks of Life and Death* (Richmond, IN: Friends United Press, 1975.

_____, *Disciplines of the Spirit.* Richmond, IN: Friends United Press, 1963.

_____, *The Growing Edge* (Richmond, IN: Friends United Press, 1956.

_____, *The Inward Journey.* New York: Harper and Row, 1971.

_____, *The Luminous Darkness.* Richmond, IN: Friends United Press, 1965.

_____, *Meditations of the Heart.* Richmond, IN: Friends United Press, 1953.

_____, *The Mood of Christmas.* New York: Harper & Row, 1973

_____, *Mysticism and Social Action: Lawrence Lectures and Discussions with Howard Thurman.* London: LARF, 2014.

_____, *The Search for Common Ground.* Richmond, IN: Friends United Press, 1971.

_____, *A Track to the Water's Edge: An Olive Scheiner Reader.* New York: Harper and Row, 1973.

_____, *Walking with God: The Sermon Series of Howard Thurman, volume one – Moral Struggle and the Prophets* (edited by Peter Eisenstadt and Walter Fluker). Maryknoll, NY: Orbis, 2020.

_____, *Walking with God: The Sermon Series of Howard Thurman, volume two – The Way of the Mystics* (edited by Peter Eisenstadt and Walter Fluker). Maryknoll, NY: Orbis, 2021.

_____, *With Head and Heart: The Autobiography of Howard Thurman.* New York: Harcourt, Brace, and Jovanovich, 1979.

Whiteheadian Texts

Daniel Dombrowski, *Process Mysticism.* Albany, NY: SUNY Press, 2023.

Bruce Epperly, *Homegrown Mystics: American Spiritual Visionaries,* Anamchara Books, 2024.

_____, *The God of Tomorrow: Whitehead on Metaphysics, Mysticism, and Mission.* Gonzalez, FL: Energion Publications, 2024.

_____, *Jesus: Mystic, Healer, and Prophet.* Anamchara Books, 2023.

_____, *Mystics in Action: Twelve Saints for Today.* Maryknoll, NY: Orbis Books, 2020.

_____, *Process Theology: A Guide for the Perplexed.* London: Continuum, 2011.

_____, *Process Theology and Mysticism.* Gonzalez, FL: Energion, 2024.

_____, *Process Theology and Politics.* Gonzalez, FL: Energion, 2020.

_____, *Process Theology and Prophetic Faith.* Gonzalez, FL: Energion, 2024.

_____, *Process Theology: Embracing Adventure with God.* Gonzales, FL: Energion, 2014.

_____, *The Mystic in You: Discovering a God-filled World.* Nashville: Upper Room Books, 2018.

_____, *We are All Mystics: How Spirituality Can Save Your Life and the World,* Anamchara Books, 2024.

_____, *The God of Tomorrow: Whitehead and Teilhard on Metaphysics, Mystics, and Mission.* Gonzales, F, 2024.L

Victor Lowe, *Alfred North Whitehead: The Man and His Work.* Baltimore: Johns Hopkins Press, 1985.

Whitehead, Alfred North. *Adventures of Ideas.* Paperback. New York: The Free Press, 1933.

_____, *The Function of Reason.* Boston: Beacon Press, 1969.

_____, Mathematics and the Good" and "Immorality," *The Philosophy of Alfred North Whitehead: Library of Living Philosophers,* volume 3, Paul Arthur Schilpp, editor. Evanston, IL: Northwestern University Press, 1941

_____, *Modes of Thought.* New York: The Free Press, 1968.

——. *Process and Reality: Corrected Edition.* Edited by David Ray Griffin and Donald W. Sherburne. New York: The Free Press, 1979.

_____, *Religion in the Making.* New York: Meridian, 1960.

_____, *Science and the Modern World.* New York: Free Press, 1967.

www.ingramcontent.com/pod-product-compliance
Lightning Source LLC
Chambersburg PA
CBHW032002080426
42735CB00007B/482